HOLOCAUST MEMORIES

ANNIHILATION AND SURVIVAL IN SLOVAKIA

PAUL DAVIDOVITS

ap

ISBN 9789493231535 (ebook)

ISBN 9789493231528 (paperback)

ISBN 9789493231740 (hardcover)

Publisher: Amsterdam Publishers, The Netherlands

info@amsterdampublishers.com

War Memories. Annihilation and Survival in Slovakia, by Paul Davidovits, is part of the series **Holocaust Survivor Memoirs WWII**

Copyright © Paul Davidovits 2021

Cover image: Paul Davidovits in his car with his dog, against a landscape of chaos during the Slovak National Uprising.

All Rights Reserved. No part of this publication may be reproduced or transmitted in any form or by any means, electronic or mechanical, including photocopy, recording or any other information storage and retrieval system, without prior permission in writing from the publisher.

CONTENTS

Prologue	1
1. My Mother's Family	5
2. My Mother and her Sisters	23
3. My Father and his Family	32
4. Early Memories	42
5. Humenne	50
6. Hungary	70
7. Out of Hungary	89
8. On the Run	102
9. Bratislava	124
10. Rakša	134
11. Back into the World	144
12. In Canada	165
Epilogue	178
Acknowledgments	181
Notes	183
About the Author	185
Amsterdam Publishers Holocaust Library	189

PROLOGUE

In the spring of 1944, when I was eight years old, I left Humenne for the last time. At that time Humenne was a small town in eastern Slovakia with a population of about 7,000 of whom, before World War II – according to the pre-war census – 2,172 were Jews.

Although the town was small, it was a regionally important commercial center, and Jews were a pivotal part of the town's centrality. A large fraction of the doctors, dentists, teachers, lawyers, and engineers were Jews. Jews also ran much of commerce, and industry. My stepfather (whom, from here on, I will call "father") owned a lumber mill that manufactured cross-ties for railroads. My maternal grandfather was a dentist.

Antisemitism was rife and the government of the newly created Slovakia eagerly modeled German antisemitic laws and participated in the annihilation of Jews. By May of 1944, about 85 percent of Slovak Jews had been deported to concentration camps where most of them were murdered. The 15,000 or so Jews remaining in Slovakia had obtained a variety of exemptions from deportation, based primarily on their importance to the Slovak economy.

Now, in the spring of 1944, with the war close to being lost by Germany and its allies, the decision was made to push for the final annihilation of all the Jews in Slovakia. As a first step toward deportation, all Jews remaining in east Slovakia had to move immediately to the western part of the country. Earlier, in preparation for what we knew was inevitably coming, my parents had bought from a forger false identifications, so-called Arian papers, for future use. With her permission, my mother used the identity of an unmarried young woman, Anna Hritzakova, who had worked for us. I was entered as her nephew, Pavel Hritzak, her brother's son.

Very clearly etched in my memory is the tension of the evening before our departure. Each of us could take only a small suitcase that my parents packed. With curtains drawn, my parents inked their fingers and stamped their fingerprints on the false documents. Then carefully they cleaned their hands to remove traces of ink. We knew that all our belongings left behind would be confiscated or stolen. My mother chose only one item to save: an album of family photographs. Our neighbor agreed to safeguard the album, and also to take care of my little terrier dog, Pityu.

That next May morning we boarded the train for Topoľčany, a city in the western part of Slovakia. We then traveled by taxi to a small village near Topoľčany where my uncle Karči and aunt Manci moved earlier to be the sole dispensers of dental care.

The first Jews came to Humenne in the early 1700s. Now after more than 200 years, we, the last of the Jews here, were leaving, expelled. The Torah scrolls from the Humenne synagogues were on the train with us. Somehow, they were lost, and did not survive the war.

The train was crowded with passengers trying to find a place for their baggage. Looking out the window, I saw Pityu running up and down the platform trying to find us. As the train pulled out of the station, Pityu started to run alongside the train. The train accelerated, and Pityu jumped down from the platform and ran alongside the train as hard as he could. The train sped up and gradually Pityu, still running, was left behind in the distance.

My mother and I were among the small remnant of Jews that survived the war. My father was killed as were most of the members of my extended family. In August of 1945, after the war had ended, my mother went back to Humenne. The house was occupied by strangers; all our possessions were gone. The neighbor returned the photo album intact and told my mother that Pityu came back the evening of our departure, stopped eating, and after a few days died. My mother then returned to Košice where we now lived with my uncle Ernő (Ernest), my mother's brother. His wife and young son had been killed. My mother remarried in 1947, and in 1949, we immigrated to Canada. When she died in 1975, the photo album passed on to me.

For the past 40 years, this old photo album has been on the back of a shelf in our living room. From time to time, I take it off the shelf and look at the pictures, some of them now more than 100 years old. Of all the people appearing in these pictures, I believe I am the only one still alive. I am the only person left who recognizes most of them, remembers how they were interconnected, and knows anything about their journey through life. I am the sole carrier of the memories these pictures contain, though even I cannot identify many of the people in the photographs. I wish I had asked my mother to fill in the blanks, but that opportunity is long gone.

With each year, the pictures get yellower and more cracked, with the images gradually fading. I have scanned some of them, specifically those of people I remember. I will try to enliven them through the memories of the child that I was when I knew these people and heard their stories. I hope the photos will regain some of their meaning, bring life to the history of my family and help me describe the improbable journey of my own survival.

1

MY MOTHER'S FAMILY

My mother's family (circa 1928).

The photograph of my mother's family was tucked between the cover and the first page of the album. In the front row, from right to left, are my maternal grandmother, her father, my aunt Erzsi (Elizabeth), at the time of the photograph still a teenager, and my mother's father Heinrich Braun. In the second row, again from right to left, are the oldest of the daughters, my aunt Manci (Margaret), my mother Rozsi (Rose) and my four uncles, Laicsi (Louis), Béla, Miklos and Ernő (Ernest). I think the self-imposed pressure on middle-class Jews to assimilate is often expressed in the specifically German and Hungarian given names.

My grandfather came to Humenne from Budapest, Hungary in the late 1800s to take over a dental practice from a retiring dentist. At that time, Humenne was still in the Hungarian part of the Austro-Hungarian Empire, so his lack of fluency in Slovak was not a serious barrier to such a move. I did not know my grandfather. He suffered from chronic asthma and died from a severe attack in the early 1930s, before I was born in 1935.

I have met three of my four uncles, all my three aunts, and my grandmother. I remember all of them except my grandmother, who died before I was a year old. I will tell as much as I know about the members of the family.

First my uncles. Their lives were not deeply intertwined with mine. Still, in my family they were a frequent subject of conversation.

The Brothers (my uncles)

Miklos (Charlie). The event imprinted as one of my earliest memories is connected to Miklos. I am about two and a half years old and am playing on the floor of our kitchen in Moldava. My mother is splitting open peapods and dropping the peas into a pot. One of the peas slips out of her hand and drops on the floor next to me. I pick it up and push it deep up my nose. My mother looks for the pea and notices what I have done with it. She frantically scoops me into her arms, runs out the door, toward the main street and then up the street to the office of the physician, one of two in Moldava, a close friend of our family.

There is a photo of him in the album which he gave to my mother when we left Moldava. The back of the photograph is dated 1939, but the day and month are illegible. It is inscribed in Hungarian "to remember me by" and signed somewhat illegibly "Dr Blau." Dr Blau took a sharp pointed tool, impaled the pea and pulled it out. During the time we lived in Moldava, he entered our lives many times.

Dr. Blau.

Much later I learned why the pea in my nose made my mother so frantic. When he was five years old her brother Miklos began to complain of headaches that got worse and worse. He was taken from one doctor to another finally ending up in a Košice hospital where they discovered, perhaps using a newly acquired X-ray machine, that a pea, deep in his nostril had sprouted, and its roots infiltrated the sinus cavity. The problem pea was cleared and quickly he got better. This story, passed on to my mother, and much later to me, left a permanent impression on both of us.

The family photograph was taken in the late 1920s. By that time my uncle Miklos, the oldest of the children, was long gone from the family configuration. He was expelled by my grandfather in 1911, a few years before the start of World

War I. When the family photograph was taken, a space was left open in the lineup of the brothers and subsequently a photograph of Miklos, that he sent from America, was skillfully worked into the picture.

Miklos was a difficult teenager to keep in line. At the age of 16, as the story is told, he met his high school teacher at the house of a local prostitute. When the flabbergasted teacher asked him "What are you doing here?", he answered, "The same thing you are." This was part of what was considered a long sequence of unacceptable behaviors and the next day Miklos was expelled from school.

Shortly thereafter, my grandfather dealt with him as was not uncommon in those days. He got in touch with a cousin in America and asked him to provide a temporary home for Miklos. The cousin, either because of a very good heart, or some obligation he had toward my grandfather, agreed. My grandfather packed up Miklos and took him by train to Hamburg where he put him on a boat to America.

After a few months in America, Miklos stole $500 from the cousin and disappeared. He reappeared in New York a few years after World War I with a new name Charles Brown, equipped with a pharmacist's license. What he had done during the intervening years, or how he became a pharmacist is not known to me (nor I think, to his children). There are many other blanks in my knowledge of his adventuresome life.

He paid back the $500, made peace with the cousin, and got a job in a pharmacy near Times Square. The pharmacist died a year later and Miklos, now Charlie, bought the business from the widow. The pharmacy apparently did well, but restless as he was, he sold it after a few years and moved to Chicago where he got a job as a traveling salesman and distributor for a drug company. Occasional letters kept the connection with his European family.

Miklos in America (circa 1940).

Lola and Charlie.

On one of his trips to Atlanta, he met Lola Cody then a model for a lingerie company. They fell in love, married, and settled for a while in Miami where their first daughter Jean was born. After a year or so in Miami, Charlie and his small family moved to Evansville, Indiana where Charlie owned and ran slot machines in several establishments. This enterprise was supposedly controlled by a crime syndicate, a connection that Charlie had cultivated while living in Chicago. For several years, he was doing very well in Evansville. Three more daughters were born to Lola and Charlie: Mary Anne, Kitty and Susie.

Charlie, Lola and their daughters (circa 1950).

Shortly after World War II, in 1947, while the family lived in Evansville, Charlie made his first return visit to Europe. He visited his brother Louis in Paris and then came to see us, that is the families of his three sisters and Ernő all now living in Košice. He still spoke an understandable Hungarian and that is how we communicated. My only clear memory of his visit is his repeated praise of the local ice cream. He bought ice cream for us and himself every time we went on an outing and never failed to remark that you cannot get such great ice cream anywhere in the US. With my idealized view of the US, I found that initially hard to believe. Having seen during the war the hundreds of powerful silvery American airplanes flying overhead, wreaking revenge on the German enemy, I believed everything American was the very best. But by the time Charlie came to visit us my image of America became a bit tainted. This disillusionment began with my watching the many cowboy movies shown in the local movie houses. The American heroes seemed somewhat clunky. Take for example Hopalong Cassidy, the great American cowboy hero, hiding behind a boulder, shooting dozens of bullets at the bad guys and missing his mark every time. So a superior ice cream in Košice now seemed plausible.

Some years after he returned from Europe, the political power in Evansville changed. The administration that made Charlie's gambling enterprise possible was voted out of office, and the police, under new orders, raided Charlie's enterprises and smashed his slot machines. The family then moved back to Miami where Charlie bought a pharmacy and a medical building. He was also a co-owner of some orange orchards near Miami.

Charlie was a multiple-pack smoker of Camel cigarettes, and in the late 1950s he began to exhibit symptoms of emphysema. His physician suggested a move to a drier climate and Charlie chose Asheville, North Carolina where he opened a grocery store.

Charlie and me in Košice (1947).

Charlie and Erzsi on his last visit to Košice.

His condition continued to deteriorate and in 1963 Charlie decided to undertake what I think he knew would be a goodbye visit to his family of origin. Again, he traveled to Paris, to Košice, and to Toronto, where my mother and Ernő now lived. He then came to New York to see me, my wife Judith and our baby son Michael. Charlie at this point could hardly breath, but he still chain-smoked his Camels. With a cigarette between his lips, he had to stop to rest every few steps he took. The cousin with whom he lived when he first came to America had died, but he arranged a get-together with the children and grandchildren of that family to reconnect with them and to connect them with me. Charlie and I took a taxi to a house on Long Island where we ate some hors d'oeuvres, drank some wine and tried to find some subjects to talk about. Soon it was evident that our paths had diverged and we had very little in common. After a couple of hours, we said our goodbyes and took a taxi back to Manhattan. The following day, Charley flew back to Asheville and died, I am told, a day later.

In the summer of 1968, I was at a conference in Nashville, Tennessee and I arranged to visit my North Carolina family. Kitty, Suzy and Lola still lived in Asheville and Mary Anne lived in Gastonia, few miles from Asheville. Only Jean moved away I think, to New Orleans. I took a bus from Nashville to Asheville where Kitty waited for me and drove me to their home. Even before I got into the car she asked, "Is it true that papa was Jewish?" She had just returned from Paris where she and her marine officer husband spent a week of their honeymoon. In Paris, they visited Maud, my uncle Louis' widow who told them that during the war she hid Louis. When asked why she had to hide him, Maud said, "The Germans were then deporting and killing Jews." Clearly, if Louis was Jewish, his brother Charlie must also have been a Jew.

When we drove up to their house, Lola was waiting on the porch, welcoming and warm. She was an attractive, elegant woman. Our family believed that Lola was a granddaughter of Buffalo Bill Cody. This must have been what Miklos told us. In fact, Lola later stated emphatically that she had no relationship to Buffalo Bill.

Lola also wanted from me the confirmation that Charlie was Jewish. She had a hard time assimilating this new information. Charlie had told her that he was Lutheran and descendent from Hungarian nobility. "I should have suspected this," she said. "Wherever we moved Charlie always sought out the local rabbi and became friends with him." When Charlie died, Lola paid $300 to bring in a Lutheran minister from a town 70 miles away to officiate at the funeral. "You know," Lola said, "his friend the rabbi attended the funeral, and he lives only a few blocks away."

The following day, a Sunday, we went to visit Mary Anne and her husband Tom Case in Gastonia. Lola, Kitty, Suzy and I drove to Gastonia in the car belonging to Kitty's husband who was on his way to Vietnam. I was the driver, because, as Kitty explained, when a man is around he is the one who drives. Driving to Gastonia was an interesting experience. The car had several military insignias on it. So while in New Haven there were anti-war rallies, here, on the way to Gastonia, men in oncoming cars flashed victory signs and some saluted sharply.

Mary Anne's house was full with friends and Tom's relatives waiting for us to arrive. As we walked in Kitty said loudly, "Y'all know we are Jewish?" There was a long silence and then I was hugged and greeted warmly. It was a wonderful event.

Back in Asheville, over a cup of coffee, Lola said to me, "It doesn't bother me that Charlie was Jewish. But Paul, what else do I not know about him?" "None of us knew Charlie well," I said, "but during the times I spent with him he always spoke about you. You all were always foremost on his mind and he loved you." "That is true," she said.

Bela in Paris (circa 1925).

Béla. Béla, the young man with the mustache in the family photo, was the second of my grandparents' children. After graduating from the gymnasium, shortly after World War I, Béla went to Paris to gain world experience and to learn a profession. This was a common route for Jewish young men of his generation. As I remember it, he obtained an apprenticeship in an architectural firm. He became fluent in French and enjoyed Paris greatly. He came to visit the family once a year and attended my grandfather's funeral and shiva.

Sometime in the early 1930s, to everybody's surprise, he wrote my grandmother that he had fallen in love with a young gentile French woman whom he planned to marry, and would like to bring her home to meet his family. My grandmother wrote back that if he didn't want to destroy her, he should break up with her and come home to

Humenne. It is hard for me to understand, but he complied and shortly after, returned home. Back in Humenne, the family mobilized and quickly introduced him to several eligible young Jewish women. He married a woman from Sabinov, a small town few miles from Humenne, where his father-in-law owned the town hotel. He took over the management of the hotel and shortly after had a son, my grandmother's first grandchild. I remember seeing a photograph of Béla with his young son sitting together at a table. This photo is missing; probably fell out of the album.

One Sunday morning, Béla and his son were sitting in the upstairs hotel dining room having breakfast, when the ceiling of the hotel collapsed, killing both of them. As you can imagine, my grandmother was devastated. She blamed herself for this catastrophe, and never again asked about the religion of the women my uncles married. Subsequently, two of the three remaining brothers married gentile women.

Ernő as an officer in the Czechoslovak army.

Ernő (Ernest). My uncle Ernő was the third son born to my grandparents. He was the most conventional and "well behaved" of the brothers. After finishing the gymnasium, he served in the Czechoslovak army and settled in Košice then a city of about 70,000, the second largest city in Slovakia and only about 40 miles from Humenne.

Ernő obtained a position as a clerk in the regional office of Phoenix, an Austrian insurance company, and rose very quickly within the ranks becoming a senior executive before he was 40. He married (I think in 1932) a young woman from a prominent Košice Jewish family. His new father-in-law was a successful lawyer and a judge. With his father-in-law's help Ernest bought an elegant house a few houses away from his in-laws' dwelling. In 1934, a son whom they named Gyuri (George) was born to Ernő and his wife. In the photograph of his new family, the in-laws are on the right with the two brothers-in-law bracketing Gyuri. As I remember it, the house in the background was Ernő's home.

Ernő and his wife.

My cousin Gyuri was a year older than I, and I remember visiting him several times. The photographs capture my memories of him, a withdrawn boy. We were expected to play together, but he would just sit and stare into space. On one of our visits to Košice when I was about three, we were in the sand-box in the back yard of Ernő's house with Gyuri completely inert sitting next to me. Out of frustration, I hit Gyuri on the head with my little plastic shovel, and made him cry. My uncle came running out of the house, yelling at me with great concern. He said something about Gyuri's frailty. I vaguely remember that this had something to do with aftereffects of scarlet fever. I was not brought to play with Gyuri again.

During 1938 and 1939, Germany took over the Czech part of Czechoslovakia, and Hungary annexed Carpathian Ruthenia and much of southern Slovakia including Košice. In June 1941, Germany attacked the Soviet Union. In expectation of a quick victory, Hungary joined the attack. At that time, the anti-Jewish laws in Hungary were already being enforced. Jews were not conscripted into the regular army, but were drafted into work brigades. My uncle Ernő was among those conscripted, and his brigade joined the

Hungarian army's march to Stalingrad. The Jewish work brigade was used as slave labor for the Hungarian and German armies, building roads, digging trenches, and doing a host of other back-breaking jobs. Most of the officers in charge of the brigade were members of the Arrow Cross, the Hungarian equivalent of the German SS. They were ardent antisemites and treated the Jews with intense cruelty. There are documented cases of Jewish conscripts herded into minefields to clear the path for the Hungarian soldiers.

The battle of Stalingrad was the first major defeat of the German army. Most of the Hungarian and German soldiers, including the Jewish conscripts, were killed, wounded or taken prisoner. The remnant of the Hungarian army began the long retreat back to Hungary. On foot, Ernő walked more than 1,000 miles back to Hungary. He told me of the starvation, the freezing and the death around him. Of the 10,000 Jews in Ernő's brigade, only 100 reached home. When I asked him how he managed to survive, he said that he had a very warm coat, but there was more to it than that. Ernő organized the men around him to watch one another for signs of freezing and arranged for the sharing of food when they were able to obtain some, as they passed through villages.

I saw him in April 1944, three months after he returned. I was already in the ghetto in Košice with my grandparents. When he came to see me, he looked gaunt and tired. I sat on his knees while he held me. Three weeks later, the Jewish residents of Košice were herded into the vast buildings of the brick factory to wait for cattle cars that would take them to Auschwitz.

Somehow, Ernő survived the ten months in Auschwitz, but when the gates of the concentration camp opened at the end of January 1945, he was near death with typhoid fever. He lay under a tree alongside of hundreds of other sick survivors unable to move. And what followed he considered a miracle of sorts, and so do I. His youngest sister Erzsi, also just let out of the concentration camp, happened to be walking by and she recognized him. Actually, she didn't recognize him, but rather the cap that covered most of his emaciated face. She nursed him for several weeks until he regained some strength. Then she herself caught typhoid fever and he nursed her back to health. My uncle Ernő is the only person I know who survived both the battle of Stalingrad and Auschwitz.

After a few months when they both gathered sufficient strength, they made their way back to Košice. This is where we met again and found out about the devastating losses we all suffered.

Many decades later, I frequently visited Ernő in Toronto where he lived in retirement with his wife in a six-apartment building, inhabited by members of the family. I would always find Ernő fully dressed in a suit and tie, sitting in his comfortable armchair reading a book or the local newspapers. I would say, "*Ernő bacsi*, let's go for a short walk." Invariably, his response was in Hungarian, "*Palikam draga* (my dear Paul), I have had enough walking for two lifetimes." And indeed, he never exercised, ate rich Hungarian meals, was overweight, and died peacefully at the age of 90.

During one of my visits to Toronto, Ernő told me about his last days in Košice before his deportation to Auschwitz. As I mentioned, Ernő and his family lived on the same street where his wealthy father-in-law had his villa. At this point, the Hungarian police and German troops were collecting

Jews from their homes loading them onto flat-bed trucks and taking them to a central depot, in the unused brick factory, for deportation to Auschwitz. The evening before they were deported, Ernő's father-in-law invited him and his family for dinner. Of course, the main topic was the ongoing deportation of Jews. His father-in-law spread out a map of Košice and explained to Ernő the street pattern of deportation. It was clear to him that the Jews on their street would not be deported, because they were all well-educated professionals who were fluent in German; obviously not the hoi polloi. Therefore, they were safe where they lived. "And he had me convinced," said Ernő.

Lajcsi (left) on the beach.

Lajcsi (Louis). I know least about my uncle Lajcsi. He left Czechoslovakia shortly after he finished the gymnasium when he was about 19. By that time, Béla was already well-established in Paris. Lajcsi became an apprentice to a watchmaker and shortly after finishing his apprenticeship he opened a jewelry and watch store. He married Maud who immigrated to France from England. and had two daughters whom I never met. I remember his brief visit to Košice after the war, possibly in 1947. He came alone and it was then that he told us how Maud hid him from the Germans, the French police and the ever-suspicious neighbors. He and my parents met several times after the war. Once, he came to Toronto, and they met again when both he and my parents visited Košice. I met him only once more when, in 1966 on the way to Israel, my wife, our four-year-old son and I stopped for four days in Paris. We stayed in Hotel California which had been the headquarters of the Gestapo during the war. When we were there, this was one of the most elegant hotels in Paris. Such were the economic conditions in France then, that even at my relatively low salary, we could afford to rent a large suite.

Lajcsi was very gracious. He took us sightseeing in Paris, went with us to Versailles and invited us to his apartment for lunch. I still remember the wonderful meal Maud prepared, especially the tomato salad. Lajcsi's had an enormous pride in all things French. He was a chain smoker and of course nobody made cigarettes as great as the French Gauloises and Gitanes. As a smoker at that time, I think he was right. He served us cheese as part of the lunch and he loudly proclaimed the wonder of French cheeses. I looked at the label where it was clearly written: "Product of Finland". I know I shouldn't have, but I pointed out the stated source of the cheese. Without a moment of hesitation, he said, "These things are often miss-labeled." Uncle Lajcsi died in his mid-eighties, sometime around 1985.

2

MY MOTHER AND HER SISTERS

My mother Rozsi (Rose) and all her siblings, the two sisters Manci (Margaret) and Erzsi (Elizabeth) as well as her three brothers, were born in Humenne. My mother was born on April 4th 1911. Theirs was very much a Jewish home with *kashrut* and Shabbat more or less observed.

Some Humenne-Jews were Orthodox Chasidim, but most, while practicing Jews, were assimilated into the 20th century and in many cases formed friendships with non-Jews. Through his dental practice, my grandfather and later my uncle Karči had strong connections to the community.

My mother and her friends played tennis, skated, danced the latest dances, went on hikes, attended parties and were freely courted by Jewish young men.

My mother (right) and her sister Erzsi were avid skaters.

Tennis players. The young woman on the left is my mother's older sister Manci. Standing behind her on the left is Manci's fiancé Karči (Charles).

Hiking was a favorite activity of young people, likely inspired by the wide influence of scouting and the German back-to-nature Wandervogel youth movements. The photo shows my mother with her two sisters hiking in the countryside of Humenne. Only two men are seen in the picture. Karči, the third man, is behind the camera. He was most often the photographer.

Young people also participated in a variety of theater groups putting on frequent performances of modern plays and musicals.

Another hike.

The solo person next to her is a cousin whose name I don't remember. She was killed in Auschwitz.

A musical performance. My mother is the fourth person from the right.

A favorite summer Sunday afternoon activity was strolling along the promenade in Humenne. This wide walkway with trees on one side stretched along the main street for about half a mile. Families with children, singles, Jews and non-Jews paraded in their most elegant clothing, stopping frequently to chat, catch up, and exchange news. Life seemed soft and easy in Humenne.

As I try to reconstruct my mother's youth, I realize that I don't know much about that period of her life; She did not speak much about it. In fact, I don't think much happened in the lives of young women growing up at that time. The lives of women in the social circle of my family were restricted and predictable. My mother graduated from a commercial high school and thereafter her life was mostly, one way or another, a preparation for marriage.

A group of friends. The men are unknown to me. The women are from right to left: my mother, a cousin, and my mother's sister Erzsi.

My mother learned to cook, to sew and to fatten geese by force-feeding. Although a live-in maidservant was always employed in the household, it was the task of the women in the family to fatten the goose. I remember as a little boy seeing my mother performing this task. The bird was bought at the outdoor farmer's market about a month before a festive holiday and brought home in a large covered basket. Before the force-feeding began, a copper coin was pushed down the throat of the goose into its stomach, which resulted in a large juicy liver. However, the fact that the large liver was produced by the toxic effect of copper was certainly not known to anyone in our household. The goose was then placed into a wooden cage so small that the confined bird was forced to sit motionless. The goose was removed for feeding through the top of the cage hinged to swing open. Twice a day, the bird was stuffed with corn kernels, softened by soaking in a bucket of water for several hours. To stuff the bird, my mother sat on the floor with the goose under her knees, holding the beak of the goose open and with her forefinger she then stuffed corn mush, a handful at a time, down the throat of the goose. When a kernel would get stuck in the air passage of the goose, the goose would begin to choke. This was a serious matter requiring immediate intervention. The first step was to slap sharply the head of the goose. If that didn't work my mother pulled a feather from the tail and pushed it through the goose's nostril to open the breathing passage. This always seemed to fix the problem. After three or four weeks of this daily stuffing, the goose was fully fattened and ready for the *shoichet*, the ritual slaughterer.

Side by side with this earthy training, there was also a highly romantic aspect to the life of the young women. Each girl had her personal song she selected from the Hungarian repertory of sad, somewhat morbid songs expressing unrequited yearnings. On summer evenings, a young man who wanted to show his admiration for a girl, would stand under her window and accompanied by a small Gypsy band, sing her song, so that all the neighbors could witness his adoration. The song often contained the girl's name, in some form. I have always known that my mother's song was "*Halvany Sarga Rozsa*". Its central refrain goes like: "Oh, you pale yellow rose, if you could only speak, you would tell me that life is not worth living." Then verse by verse the song elaborates the cause of the singer's despair.

Decades later, in the 1960s, when my mother was already sick with lung cancer, she came to visit us in Boston. Our whole family went to a Hungarian restaurant that featured a Gypsy orchestra. I slipped the violinist a note with a ten-dollar bill asking him to come to our table at some point and play my mother's song. The small orchestra came to the table and started to play. Tears welled up in my mother's eyes and she cried. Several versions of this song are on YouTube. I play the song from time to time and even now the sadness and the longing well up.[1]

This genre of doom-romance Hungarian songs was popular in the early 1930s, probably reflecting the hopelessness of the Great Depression, combined with the yearning of the young post-war generation. One of these songs, "*Szomoru Vasarnap*", in the English translation known as Gloomy Sunday, gained world-wide popularity and was dubbed "the suicide song", because, as legend has it, a large number of people killed themselves while this song was playing on their gramophone.[2] This romantic aspect of the young women's early lives was in fact a veneer. When it came to selecting husbands, for most young women in my mother's social group the choices were constrained. As was the custom, both my mother and her sister Erzsi married men to whom they were introduced by my uncle Ernő. The young men had been Ernő's classmates in college. They were several years older than the women, came from good families, had solid professions and good economic prospects. These men were not from Humenne and were not known to the girls prior to Ernő's introductions. I don't know if there were any dowry arrangements in these marriages. I think not, as I had not heard dowry mentioned in my family.

My aunt Erzsi married Geza Czikk, an accountant eight years her senior. He had a stable job with a well-established firm. I remember him as a colorless, quiet, and as everyone noted, very industrious man. At the time of their engagement he already owned a house and that was a major draw. The album does not contain their wedding picture, but I did find a picture of Geza and Erzsi with Miklos taken after the war when Miklos visited Košice.

My mother married Imre Davidovits whose parents lived in Moldava, a small town about 100 miles from Humenne. Moldava, situated on the river Bodva, then had a population of about 2,000 with a sizable Jewish community of about 500 people.

My aunt Manci's marriage to Karči played out somewhat differently. Manci's father Heinrich (my grandfather) was becoming increasingly incapacitated by asthma attacks. He advertised nationally for a young dentist to join him in his dental practice. Karči, from Budapest, applied and was selected for the partnership. Manci and Karči fell in love and, as I understand it, carried out their romance in secret. She became pregnant, had an abortion and soon after, they married. She was a wonderful warm woman who very much wanted children. Unfortunately, something had gone wrong with the abortion and thereafter she could not conceive.

From right to left Geza, Erzsi and Miklos.

Wedding picture of my parents, Rozsi and Imre.

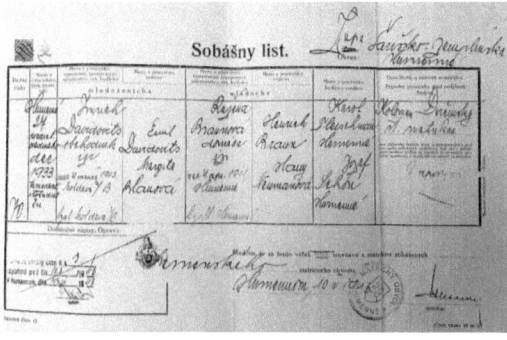

My parents' marriage certificate.

3

MY FATHER AND HIS FAMILY

I know much less about my father's family than about my mother's. After my father died in 1938, when I was not quite three years old, I lived mostly with my mother's family. Perhaps more importantly for my ability to reconstruct the past, all of my mother's siblings survived World War II, and so my contact with my mother's family continued well into my adulthood. My father's family however was all killed during the Holocaust. I am the only survivor.

My Grandfather. Emil Davidovits, my grandfather, owned a wholesale grocery store in Moldava. I remember it as a vast space with burlap bags of grains, wheat, rice, dried fruits, some opened and some sealed, rows of canned goods in orderly formations on shelves and always a wonderful scent of spices permeating the space. The store was very successful, with people coming and going all day.

In the 1920s, my grandfather built what at that time was the largest private house in Moldava. I remember the house as a beautiful structure, but modest by city standards. The store fronted the main street and the residential section was in the rear, surrounding a large garden. Part of the garden complex was a separate house and a large shed. At that time, Moldava did not have a central sewage system or central water supply. The toilets were in an outdoor building, and several wells supplied water. The kitchen had its own indoor well that supplied water for the whole house.

My grandparents' store and house in Moldava. From the postcard collection of Dalibor Danko.

During WWII, when I was seven going on eight years old, I lived with my grandparents for about one year in Moldava, which at that time was in Hungary. I remember my grandfather as a stern, but a kind man. I attended school that year and he was the one who helped me memorize the multiplication table. To this day, if I want to obtain the result of multiplying any two numbers up to 12, the result comes to me in Hungarian with his voice echoing in the background.

There was at least one of my grandfather's traits that I think I absorbed into my life. Moldava was a rich apple-growing country with a type of apple called "Jonotan" or "Jonathan" which are also grown in the northeast US. Every summer during the height of the apple harvest season, my grandfather bought a large number of apples and had them brought to the house in a wheelbarrow. The whole family then spent hours wrapping them in old newspaper sheets. These wrapped apples were stacked side-by-side on shelves in the unheated pantry. When the season turned, and apples were no longer available in the stores, my grandfather would go into the pantry after dinner and by lightly squeezing the wrapped apples he determined which had acquired soft spots and were on their way to rotting. He then picked out those that were near the end of their edible lifespan and brought them into the dining room. He gave one to each of us that we then unwrapped, cut out the soft and sometimes rotten sections and ate the remainder after dinner as part of the dessert. In this way we ate apples through the winter, but never had a really good, crisp one.

This is an approach to life that has not been easy for me to shake. I often find myself in the mode of my grandfather's apple selecting. I get new shirts and sweaters, mostly as birthday gifts, but I always feel a great reluctance to wear the new clothing, and am more likely to put on the worn, shabby ones. I am comfortable putting on the new clothing only after my old clothing is so worn-out that my wife insists that it be thrown out.

My Grandmother. I don't know much about my paternal grandmother, Margita, but I do remember her as gentle and kind. My parents' marriage certificate states that her maiden name was Margita Blau. When I was eight years old, I lived with my paternal grandparents after I spent half a year in an orphanage. When I think back to that year I spent in my grandparents' home in Moldava, it is clear that I was a very disturbed child. After having been in complete control of my bodily functions for many years, I started to urinate in bed, had nightmares and suffered insomnia. My grandmother spent many hours sitting at my bedside in the middle of the night, holding my hand and soothing me.

My grandparents had three sons and one daughter: my father Imre, my uncles Zoli and Karcsi and a daughter, whose name, I am sorry to have forgotten.

My paternal grandparents vacationing, probably in Karlove Vary.

My father Imre. I have only a few isolated memories of my father who died when I was three years old. What I know about him I learned mostly from my uncle Ernő. The two of them were classmates in college, enrolled in a program that we would call Business Administration now. It was common at that time for students to purchase a meal ticket from a local restaurant for a number of meals covering most of the academic year. Ernő and Imre ate most of their dinners together. At times, they were joined by other students and sometimes by visiting parents. Ernő told me that these meals were an important part of their social lives where connections were formed that lasted well past their college years.

My father is the first man in the second row.

Visiting Humenne. From right to left: a great aunt, my father, my mother and grandmother holding me, my aunt Manci.

Ernő told me that my father Imre was one of the top students, a quiet man, with an excellent sense of humor. According to my mother he was a kind man who doted on me. Some things can be deduced about him from the few photographs in the album. Comparing him to the other people in the existing photographs, I estimate he was about six feet in height, tall by the standards of the day. While the others in the photo are smiling, he is serious and appears aloof.

The last of the three photos I have of my father in a group setting, I think it was taken in Ruthenia where his sister lived with her family. They all seem to be admiring someone outside of the picture, probably a baby. Here my father is in fact smiling.

Father in Ruthenia.

My Uncle Zoli. The oldest son, Zoli, had a physical handicap which may have been a mild form of cerebral palsy. His walk was spastic, with his left foot dragging behind the leading right foot. Often little children followed him on the street, walking behind him, imitating his walk. I liked my uncle Zoli and I remember that the children making fun of him behind his back very much bothered me. He worked in the store with my grandfather who seemed perpetually dissatisfied with him.

Zoli's wife Zsuzsi (Susan) was a beautiful woman. They had two daughters, both younger than me. Zoli, with his family, lived in the separate house within the compound of my grandfather's house. When I lived with my grandparents, I remember spending a lot of time with Zoli and his family. At that time, I was deeply immersed in American cowboy and Indian stories. I read all the translated adventure stories of the American West I could obtain, mostly by Fennimore Cooper, Charles May and Zane Grey. My potential supply of such books was doubled, because I could read them both in Slovak and in Hungarian.

One afternoon, both Zoli and Zsuzsi were away and I was alone with my two little cousins in their kitchen. My older cousin, Marika, was about six and the younger a toddler of about three. I convinced my older cousin to play cowboys and Indians and while she held the toddler I tied her up in her highchair and we both ran around her making what I thought were Indian whooping noises. She did not seem to mind. She just sat there and watched us with interest. When Zsuzsi came in through the door I was in serious trouble. My grandfather was called to take in the scene. I was yelled at, made to apologize and promise never to do such a thing again. I kept that promise. I never tied up any babies in a high chair again.

Soon I was forgiven. Zsuzsi in fact liked me very much. One day, she had a pain in her abdomen. She made an appointment with the family doctor and took me with her as her chaperon. We sat in the doctor's office, but, out of modesty, she did not want him to touch her. The doctor handed her a large doll and she pointed to the place where the pain was localized and answered several questions about the pain. He then wrote a prescription and we left.

Zoli and Zsuzsi's older daughter Marika.

My Uncle Karcsi. (Charles) Karcsi, my grandparents' youngest son, was a very handsome man. He was the head of the local Esperanto club and seemed always to be reading and brooding. I have two clear memories of him. I am about two or two-and-a-half years old and am sitting on the stone stairs leading into the store. My uncle Karcsi is leaning against the wall adjacent to the stairs and is eating a lemon, skin and all. I know the sour taste of lemons and am amazed to see him eat it. In my other memory, which is situated around the same time period, it is Shabbat after noon and I am sitting on the wooden bench in the large kitchen of my grandparent's house. The house is quiet. People are napping. My uncle Karcsi enters the kitchen. He sees me, and sits down next to me. I ask him to tell me a story. He pulls out his penis and answers that he will if I take his penis into my mouth. That is where the memory ends. I don't recall whether I did as he asked or if, he told me a story.

In 1943, a few weeks after I came from the orphanage to Moldava, Karcsi was drafted into the forced Jewish labor battalion of the Hungarian army. The Jewish young men conscripted into the "battalion" were simply slave laborers, without uniforms, without weapons, guarded by sadistic antisemitic Hungarian soldiers. Their main job was to dig trenches and repair roads. They were poorly fed and very badly treated.

My father's youngest brother Karcsi.

I don't know how I learned about my uncle Karcsi's death. Probably someone who survived the horrible ordeals of those times recounted what occurred. In the confusion of the battle of Stalingrad, Karcsi, with several other young men, managed to escape and crossed the battle line into Soviet held territory. They were quickly placed under arrest and extensively questioned. Having told the arresting Russian soldiers that they were Jews and communist sympathizers, they expected to be welcomed. Instead, they were herded into a concentration camp together with other Hungarian and German prisoners of war. Their treatment was brutal and merciless. Karcsi became deeply despondent and after several days in the camp hurled himself onto the electrified fence and died.

My Father's Sister. My father's only sister, I believe her name was Ilona, married Lajcsi (Louis) Korach who was a pharmacist in Hust, a small town in Ruthenia which was part of Czechoslovakia, then Hungary and now Ukraine. They had three sons, Otto, Gyuri and Laci.

My three cousins from Hust, from right to left: Otto (the oldest), Gyuri and Laci.

4

EARLY MEMORIES

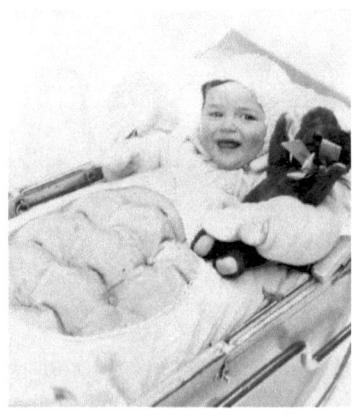

Me at 15 months.

I was born November 1, 1935 in Moldava nad Bodvou ("Moldava on the river Bodva") which was then part of Czechoslovakia. At the time of my birth, about 2,000 people lived in Moldava of whom about 500 were Jews. The town is about 20 miles from Košice, the second largest city in Slovakia.

My mother, while pregnant, had read about a case in a US hospital where two babies were mislabeled and had been taken home by the wrong parents. Then and there, my mother decided she was not going to subject her future child to such a risk and even though most of her friends were arranging for hospital births she gave birth to me at home with the assistance of a midwife and our family physician on call.

My memories begin in 1938 when I was about two-and-a-half years old. Few of these early memories are attached to specific time-traceable events, but most are free floating of time.

Shortly after the event of the pea up my nose, I came down with scarlet fever. Before the advent of antibiotics, this streptococcal infection was a serious, often fatal disease. I was kept in bed for two weeks in a darkened room. The belief was that the disease made the eyes particularly sensitive to light with possible damage to vision. There may have been some validity to that practice, but I am sure that my diet was far less evidence-based. For two weeks, I was fed mostly kimmel soup, a Hungarian-Jewish healing specialty with caraway seeds and potatoes as its main ingredient. The soup made me gag, but I knew that I had to get it down if I were to get better. When my uncles, aunts and neighbors came to visit, which they did every day, my first question to them was always, "What did you have for dinner?" They were all instructed to respond: "Kimmel soup". Of course, I knew this was not the case and we all laughed at this mutually agreed on joke. I remember these episodes as the only cheerful times of my endless two weeks in bed.

The album contains several photos that were taken during our occasional visits to Humenne where my grandmother and my aunt Manci with her husband Karči lived. These photos I am quite certain were taken by Karči.

Visiting my grandmother in Humenne.

When I turned two, my mother started to work in my grandfather's wholesale grocery store. At this point my father had already been working there as an outside salesman. My mother hired a nanny to take care of me while she worked in the store. The nanny was a tall thin woman and we did not get along at all. I did not want her to take care of me; I wanted my mother. She always seemed to be yelling at me for one reason or another. On one occasion, she was toilet training me and forced me to sit on a white porcelain chamber pot. I did push out some feces, and then I took a pile of dominoes and threw them on top of the bowel movement in the pottie. My guess is that I had done something like this before, because I knew this made her angry. She would have to retrieve the dominoes and clean them. This time, she picked out the domino pieces, washed them off, then picked me up and slammed me into my baby carriage and wheeled me to the store. She deposited me in front of my mother, and quit.

My mother stopped working in the store and stayed home with me.

My aunt Manci giving me a bath.

Another memory. It is Saturday afternoon, and I am in the back yard alone while my parents are napping in the bedroom. I am bored and I want them to pay attention to me. I know that I can't just go into their bedroom and ask to join them. They will tell me to leave. I devised a plan; I took my little wheelbarrow, opened the gate in the fence and went out on the sidewalk. I walked to the small grocery store about a block away where my parents bought fruits and vegetables. The grocer of course knew me and greeted me with delight. I saw in a large wooden crate a pile of melons. I told the grocer that my mother had sent me to get a melon. He picked out a melon, put it into my barrel and I wheeled the wheelbarrow into my parents' bedroom. As they sat up in their bed, I told them that I brought them the melon as a present. This of course had the planned effect. They were delighted with me; how smart, how cute. I heard the recounting of this event several times.

During the summer of 1938, my three cousins, Otto, Gyuri and Laci Korach, the sons of my father's sister, were visiting us from Hust, a small town now in Ukraine, but then part of Czechoslovakia. Otto is about eight years old, Gyuri seven and Laci about six. My cousins and I are in my grandparents' garden while the adults are indoors. My grandparents' old big black dog Bobi is following us as we are running around. At one point, the cousins decided to play with the dog, but the play soon degenerated into tormenting him by pulling his ears and tail. The dog yelped, but did not resist. I became very upset. I yelled at them, I cried but they would not stop. After so many years, I can still get in touch with the frustration and anger. I decided to leave home, so I opened the gate connecting the garden to the street, and walked out and up along the main street. I was walking for what seemed a long time, when a policeman came up to me, picked me up and carried me back to my grandparents' house. I was reprimanded and I had to promise not ever to walk out on the street by myself. This was not the only time that my three cousins brought me trouble.

That summer in 1938, my father took me by train to Košice, about a half-an-hour ride, to visit the regional fair. Impending war with Germany was now a frequent topic of conversation. I remember clearly walking next to my father holding his hand. As we walked through the gate to the fairground, I looked to my right and on a raised platform I saw a horrifying sight; a figure wearing a black mask with a hose extending to a cylinder on his belt. I screamed. My father picked me up, reassured me and told me that this was a soldier in a gas mask and with weapons to show that our country will be safe from enemies.

Our first stop at the fair was the electric bumper-car ride. That was amazing. Little cars riding round and round, smashing into each other. My father bought a ticket for us. Even now I can summon up the feeling of sitting in his lap and steering erratically while he controlled the speed. We are bumping and being bumped and laughing and laughing.

My Father's Death

Toward the end of summer 1938, my father became sick with a severe sore throat and high fever. I remember him lying in bed, always with a pitcher of lemonade on the night table. The doctor came to visit every day, but my father was not getting better. Then one day, a whole group of people came to our house – family, friends and some people I had never met. They were milling around and talking in whispers. It was clear that there was a problem. Nobody was paying any attention to me. I remember being very upset, probably because everybody was so perturbed. I cried and someone gave me a glass of lemonade from the pitcher on the night table. The family was gathered around my father's bed: my mother my grandfather, my grandmother, my father's two brothers Karcsi and Zoli. I was not allowed to come near the bed, but could stay in the bedroom. Then an ambulance arrived from Košice. Two men with a stretcher came into the bedroom. My grandmother took me by the hand and led me out of the bedroom. My father was taken out on the stretcher and put into the ambulance, while my mother got in with him. The ambulance drove off and I stayed with my grandparents. After five days my mother returned home.

I am outside on the street walking on the sidewalk. In a small town like Moldava, children – even my age – could walk freely outdoors. Very few cars traveled the streets and people drove carefully, mindful of little children. I see my mother running toward me. I run to meet her. I am aware of the grassy bank on the side of the paved street. As I am running I realize that I am urinating in my pants. My mother embraces and hugs me. Nobody ever told me that my father Imre died. I suppose the notion was that if they did not say anything I may not notice.

In fact, I believe I knew that he died before my mother came back from Košice. Likely, I sensed the mood and probably I heard my grandparents or uncles talking about his death. But for a long time my father was not mentioned in my presence.

Now, I know that he died of a streptococcal infection that started in his throat and then attacked his heart. That was quite common then. A streptococcal infection is now completely stopped by a course of antibiotics, but in those days it was often fatal.

In the early 2000s, my daughter Deborah and her husband Matt visited Slovakia where, in the Košice Jewish cemetery, they found my father's grave. They made a less than perfect rubbing using grass and individual sheets of paper showing part of his Hebrew and Hungarian names and the years of his birth and death.

A rubbing of my father's gravestone.

5

HUMENNE

In late fall of 1938, in a deal brokered by Nazi Germany, Czechoslovakia was split into the Czech part, which in effect was ruled by Germany, and the Slovak part, that became the Fascist state of Slovakia. Hungary took over southern Slovakia that included Košice and Moldava. Humenne, where my mother was born and many of her friends lived including her sister Manci and her husband Karči, remained part of Slovakia.

There was now not much in Moldava to keep my mother there, and she decided to return to Humenne. Manci and Karči had a thriving dental practice and had a place for us to live. Of course, we had to get a passport, because Humenne was now in a different country. The picture taken for our joint passport is shown below.

Passport photo, 1939.

In 1939 we returned to Humenne. On the way we stopped overnight in Košice, where my uncle Ernő and aunt Erzsi lived with their families. We stayed in Ernő's house which was bigger than Erzsi's and had spare bedrooms. I remember that after my father's death I became fearful and would not go to sleep alone. My mother had to come with me to the bedroom and I would fall asleep holding her elbow. In Košice that evening, we were sitting in the large living room when my mother said that it was time for me to go to sleep. I slid off the chair and my mother stood up to come with me. My uncle said to her. "You should let him go to sleep by himself, otherwise you will spoil him." Not giving in to children's fears was at that time, the common wisdom of child rearing. Walking out the door, without turning, my mother said to him, "Don't be stupid."

We arrived in Humenne by train and my aunt and uncle, Manci and Karči, were waiting for us on the platform as the train pulled in. My mother got off first and she helped me down from the train. Manci scooped me up and hugged and kissed me. Thereafter she has always been a loving presence in my life.

The nature of memories, that is, what and how we remember, remains a mystery. How is it that I have clear memories between the ages two and three, while we lived in Moldava, but the first two years in Humenne, when I was between 3 and 5 years old, have left me with almost no memories? Was it the death of my father or perhaps the dislocation from my home in Moldava that turned off that part of me that retains memories and makes them accessible? Only one event from that time period left a clear imprint. Shortly after our arrival in Humenne, my mother and I are visiting a friend of hers. The two of them are sitting in the garden at a metal table talking and drinking some beverage in a glass. I am standing next to my mother. A bowl of fruit is on the table and my mother hands me an apple. A group of four boys, older than I am, perhaps five or six years, comes into the garden. They are rowdy and are playing some type of a game. My mother seems to know them and greets them. One of them comes over and asks me to join them in their game. I am delighted to join, and my mother encourages me to do so. The group, now five of us, makes our way through some bushes to an adjacent garden. The boys tell me that in this game I will be blindfolded and given a stick. They will then keep calling out while I chase them around the garden following their voices. If I get to hit one of them I will win, and the person I hit will take my place. I am blind folded and the stick is extended toward me. I take hold of the extended end of the stick and I quickly realize that the stick is coated with some sticky stinking matter. I pull off the blindfold and see that the end of the stick I am holding is coated with excrement. I feel betrayed and furious. I try to chase them, but they can run faster and disappear. I sob uncontrollably while my mother cleans me up and we go home. Searching for other memories, I try to visualize or transpose myself into that time space of 1939 to 1940, but aside from that one unpleasant, painfully enraging event nothing else is brought forth.

I do know that sometime during this period my Uncle Karči built a functioning toy car for me. Looking at a photograph of the car, I realize that this was a remarkable construction. He used the wheels of my baby carriage for the wheels of the car and he bent sheet metal to make the car body. The car had a functioning steering wheel and pedals for propelling it forward. He painted the car red. Obviously it was a beautiful child's car, but I don't remember whether I was delighted with it. Most likely I was; how could I not have been?

Soon after we arrived in Hummene, my mother renewed contact with a previous acquaintance, Ignac Mandel. I don't know who initiated the contact, but I remember liking him from the very first time I met him. He was 37 years old and a bachelor. Shortly after he and I met, he took me to see the large saw mill that he owned, where trees were converted to railroad crossties. He explained that he bought a forest, his crew cut down the trees that were suitable for crossties and the trees were brought to the lumber yard for processing. I was fascinated by the large machines that made huge noises. In the fall of 1940, my mother and he were married and I had a new father who became truly a father to me. I became very attached to him. I remember asking my mother if it would be possible for me to look like Ignac. She looked at me and said, "No you cannot look like Ignac, but you can be like him."

Ignac Mandel.

Ignac and my mother on the beach.

Ignac had a large family that became also my family. His mother and father were still alive and immediately treated me as their new grandson. His two brothers and sister who lived in Humenne became my new uncles and aunt and their children my cousins. I remember spending a lot of time with my father Ignac. At times he took me with him on his trips to see the forest he was planning to buy. Most Saturdays he and I went together to the steam bath that was built by the Jewish community adjacent to the Jewish school. One afternoon he came home and without a word he handed me a shoebox. I sat down on the floor, took off the cover and saw a little puppy in the box. "That is your dog." He said to me. I named the dog Pityu (Pete). I loved him.

Pityu

Many of my memories from this time are centered around my Grandfather Mandel, the father of Ignac. He was a farmer, one of the few Jewish farmers in the area. He had a small farm at the edge of Humenne, a short ride on my bicycle from the center of town where we lived. In his fields he grew wheat and corn. He had a small herd of cows, about ten of them, some chickens, ducks, and a few rabbits in cages. He also had two horses that were used to pull a wagon. He was a highly respected member of the region's farmer community.

Grandfather Mandel was missing one eye, with only a hollow socket in its place. He had a glass eye that he showed us but he never used it. Later my father told me that in his youth Grandfather Mandel was a champion in the use of the whip. In such competitions you crack the long whip as you aim at a distant target. The tip of the whip is maneuvered back and forth as it zeroes in on the target. In one such competition, the returning whip hit his eye and injured it so severely that it had to be taken out.

My cousins and I, seven of us, both boys and girls, spent a lot of time playing on my new grandfather's farm. Many interesting things held our attention there. Next to the barn where the cows lived was a big pile of hay. Using a ladder propped to the side of the barn, we would climb on the roof then jump into the pile of hay below. There was always a lot of laughter and squealing. Our grandfather gave us chores to do; feeding the cows, the chickens, the ducks, petting the rabbits. These little chores were converted to games. Some afternoons grandfather hitched the two horses to the wagon and we would all climb aboard, ride around in the wagon, each one of us taking a turn controlling the reins. It was evident that he loved us and really enjoyed having us with him.

One afternoon grandfather's farmhand didn't show up and he asked me to herd the cows to the pasture, some distance away. Going there was easy. The cows knew where to go. I had a little stick and only occasionally did I have to swat one of the cows that was lagging behind. We walked along the dirt path until we came to the meadow where the cows started to eat the grass. Grandfather gave me an old pocket watch and told me to bring the cows back after an hour of grazing. When the time came, I started to herd the cows for the return trip and at first all went well. We started off on the same path that brought us to the pasture. Then we came to a fork and I didn't know which path to take. The cows decided for me. Half the herd went right, the other half to the left. I panicked; no idea what to do. At this point I was no longer herding. I just followed one of the paths, hoping that at least this group was heading in the right direction. I was really scared. It looked like I lost half of grandfather's herd. The barn came into view, and my half of the herd headed right in. And there in the barn were the other cows already waiting. Grandfather came out of the house. "Well done", he said.

Among farmers in those days there was a custom of *zabíjačka*. Literally the word means "killing", but there is a festive connotation to it. Before winter set in, usually in late fall, one of the family pigs would be slaughtered and the various parts of the pig would be prepared for winter consumption. Some of the meat would be smoked, other parts would be made into sausage that would be stored in a barrel with lard from the pig, poured over the layers of sausage to preserve it. Some of the meat would be saved for a festive meal and a party to which neighbors would be invited. My grandparents were strictly kosher and of course they would not eat pork. Still often they would be invited to a *zabíjačka* celebration. My grandfather Mandel took me to one of these, an event that I still remember very clearly. A small Gypsy orchestra played music, and men and women danced and sang. Grandfather didn't dance or eat but he talked with his neighbors and drank vodka. From time to time, one of the men hoisted one of us boys on his shoulder, danced, jumped around, and twirled.

Bicycling in Humenne.

In my car with Pityu.

Those days in 1940 and 1941 were truly a halcyon time in my life. I had everything a child of that time could want: a loving family, a bicycle, a car, a dog, a group of playmates, and absorbing activities. In September 1941, I was enrolled in the first grade of the Humenne public school and in the afternoon I attended Hebrew school. I went to school carrying a small bag with a shoulder strap that contained my new notebook. I very much liked going to school, joining the big kids.

Periodically, during the summer, a polio epidemic would sweep our town and of course the whole region. At the first sign of polio, most of the mothers in our circle of friends, took their children and traveled by train to some remote spa in the mountainous region where we would spend a few weeks until the epidemic subsided. These times away were endless days of boredom. Our mothers played cards all day and we children wandered around aimlessly looking for things to do. One day we found a bird on the ground barely moving. Somewhere we obtained a shoebox and placed the bird on some leaves. We dug out worms from the ground and placed them next to the bird's head, thinking that the food will revive it but next morning the bird was dead. We dug a small grave and buried the bird. That was a highlight of that year's stay in the spa.

The serious consequence of polio was not explained to me nor was I aware of it until I personally observed it. A neighbor, a few houses from ours, was a physician (I don't remember his name), with a son, about my age who was a friend. The physician was experimenting with some type of anti-polio vaccine that he developed. We all knew about his research, but nobody took it seriously. The physician however, had great confidence in his work and injected his son with the vaccine. When the polio epidemic in the summer of 1941 struck, we traveled to the resort near Bardejov, but the physician kept his son in Humenne. When the epidemic subsided, we returned home and learned that the physician's son contracted polio and was nearly completely paralyzed. I recall visiting him once. He lay motionless on his bed. He could speak, and we talked a bit, but I found the visit very awkward. I certainly did not know how to respond to his predicament.

I don't remember my mother being especially superstitious, but an event stands out. One afternoon a man my mother knew, came to visit. He was a big man with a fat face and big belly. I don't remember the season, but it must have still been cold, because he wore a large coat that he took off. We all sat in the living room, the visitor at one end of the sofa and my uncle Karči and aunt Manci on the other end, with a space separating them. My mother and I sat on chairs opposite them. Between us was a coffee table with a plate of cookies and a pitcher, I think, of lemonade. My father was not with us. The conversation was boring and I paid no attention to it. After some time my mother suddenly got up from her chair took me by the hand and led me out of the room into the bath room. She pulled down my pants and told me to urinate into her palm. There was urgency in her voice and I did as she told me. She quickly washed my face with my urine, some of it dripping on the floor. She told me that this was to protect me from the visitor who wished me ill. I had no idea what she meant. She wiped the floor, and we quickly returned to the living room. She never talked about this episode, nor did she ever do this again. Many years later, already in my adulthood, I learned that washing the face of a child with urine was an old East European Jewish method for keeping the evil eye from harming a child.

My idyllic world began to collapse in the late fall of 1941, when grandfather Mandel died suddenly of a heart attack. On the day of his death, his corpse covered with a white sheet was laid out on the table in the living room of his house. We, the children, were free to roam. I remember we gathered around the corpse and one of the boys uncovered grandfather's right foot. We took turns pinching his big toe to see if he would move, until an adult came in and chased us out.

The Slovak fascist party took over the country in 1939, and in September of 1941 they began to enact a range of antisemitic laws called the Jewish Code, modeled closely on the German anti-Jewish legislation. Jews had to wear yellow armbands, could not hold government jobs, and could not work as teachers or professionals, except under special circumstances. Intermarriage between Jews and non-Jews was strictly forbidden. In 1940, through a process called arianization, 51 percent of the ownership of Jewish firms was forcefully transferred to non-Jews. Soon after, all Jewish businesses were confiscated. After nearly 100 years of service to the Jewish community, my Jewish school was forced to close. On the day of its closing teachers, students, and parents gathered in front of the school. My father held my hand. Some people made speeches and then the group sang a sad Slovak song traditional for students graduating from a school. I still remember the first words of the song, *Goodbye school we are departing.* Many people cried, including my father.[1]

Initially the Jewish Code stipulated that Jews who converted to Christianity before 1939 were exempt from these laws. A Greek Orthodox priest in Humenne was willing to forge documents for Jews, entering a false date into the records to show that the conversion took place before 1939. For adults, he was willing to do this without any actual conversion ceremonies. However, he insisted that a child receiving such a documentation must undergo a regular Church approved conversion process.

My father and mother took me to the church, and I remember kneeling at the altar in the empty church, with my head bowed over a silver bowl while the priest, reciting some prayers, poured holy water on my head. He taught me how to cross myself in the Greek Orthodox manner which, as he pointed out to me, is different from the way Roman Catholics cross themselves.

As I remember it, the night of my conversion, or very shortly after, I had a dream that after nearly eighty years, still haunts me. I am in a large meadow surrounded by Jews dressed in the traditional black garb of the Orthodox. In front of me, at the end of the meadow, is a huge mountain. Suddenly, the black garbed Jews start running away from me. I see in horror that the mountain sprouts hands holding a giant mountain-sized ax. The ax is raised and it comes down on top of my head, splitting me in half. I wake up in horror.

Still, I did not want to be a Jew anymore. I wanted to be a Christian. I remember clearly, a recruiter from the Hlinka Guard, the Fascist Slovak youth organization, the Fascist analogue of the cub scouts, came to our classroom recruiting for the youth group. He showed us the uniforms we would get as members; the shirt, the cap, the belt. The whole class signed up. I wanted to belong as well and I put my name on the list. We were to meet in the afternoon, in the back yard of the local Hlinka guard headquarters for initiation. After school I went home and told my parents that I wanted to join the Hlinka youth group and attend on the afternoon for which I signed up. They looked very conflicted, but then my mother and father consulted and agreed to let me go.

The boys in our class were lined up in the back yard of the Hlinka Guard headquarters (only boys were recruited) and one by one each boy was called up alphabetically by an adult leader dressed in the forbidding black uniform. Each boy went up to the leader and was handed a shirt, cap and belt and was then directed to line up closer to the building for the initiation ceremony. Soon, it became clear to me that my name was skipped. Finally, all the boys were called up and they marched toward the building entrance laughing and jeering at me. I was left alone in the yard feeling embarrassment and shame. I can still feel the graveled composition of the back yard as I walked through the gate onto the street. When I got home, my parents didn't ask, and I didn't tell them what happened.

My hope to become a Christian continued. Whenever we passed a church I crossed myself. When we went on outings in my uncle's car and passed the ubiquitous road-side cross with the crucified Jesus I would cross myself and mumble the required short prayer, but I would do this secretly, because I was ashamed of doing so; I would duck low where I thought nobody in the car could see me.

Christmas was approaching. Since I wanted to have a Christmas tree, my parents brought home a small pine tree a week before Christmas and decorated it with lights and trinkets. The next day, in school, the priest who converted me, and one of the teachers asked me if we had a Christmas tree in our house. I said proudly that we did. He looked at me and said that he did not believe me.

Soon, it became evident that it would not be possible for me to become a Christian. In fact, just a few months after the exemption for converts was announced, it was retracted. There were now no exemption for Jews, converted or not.

In March of 1942, deportation of Slovak Jews to concentration camps in German held territories began. Quotas were set on the number of Jews to be deported each week. According to a variety of sources, the Fascist Slovak government, in effect, outsourced the murder of its Jewish population by paying the German Nazi government for each Jew taken out of Slovakia to German controlled camps, ostensibly for resettlement. The amount of payment quoted in several available sources was in the range of several thousand German Marks. In return for the payment, the Germans guaranteed that the removal of Jews was permanent. The Slovak government recouped some of the cost of deportation by taking possession of the vacated Jewish properties. About 15% of the Jews, those who were considered essential to the Slovak economy, were issued official exemption permits sparing them from deportation. My father and our small family were granted such an exemption. Although he no longer owned the company, his expertise was required to run the saw mill.

An event from one of the first rounds of deportation, is sadly in my mind. Our physician neighbor, who experimented with the polio vaccine, did not get an exemption from deportation. My guess is that an exemption was denied to him because with his paralyzed son he could not relocate to some remote village where physicians were needed. When someone ran to our house to tell us that the physician and his family were being deported, I immediately ran to the physician's house to see what was happening. In front of the house a flatbed truck was parked, already with several families and their baggage loaded on it. Suitcases of the physician were being passed to men standing on the flatbed. And then I saw the physician emerging from the house, cradling the limp body of his son in his arms walking toward the truck. The boy's hands and feet were dangling motionlessly by his side. He lifted his son's body and laid it on the flatbed. I ran to the truck and saw that my friend was crying. I said goodbye to him, but he did not answer.

As the year 1942 progressed, deportation of Jews continued, and having exemption documents was no longer a guarantee of safety. The local police and Hlinka Guard were periodically ordered to round up a certain number of Jews for deportation. As the Jewish population declined, at times, even those with exemptions were caught in the net and deported. My father had acquaintances in the police department who usually alerted him when a deportation action was about to be implemented. We would then go into hiding in the attic of a gentile friend and stay there till we were told that the train carrying the deportees had departed. As I remember it, such deportation actions occurred about once a week.

After one such deportation action I came down from the attic where we were hiding and joined a group of Jewish boys wandering through our town looking through the windows of houses from which families had been deported. By the time we got there, the houses had already been ransacked with most of the things that were worthwhile already stolen.

While wandering we came to the small house of the ritual slaughterer, the *shoichet* of Humenne. We all knew the man, because at one time or another we would carry a chicken, a duck or even a goose to his house to be ritually slaughtered following the laws of *kashrut*. This was often a task of the boys in the family. The *shoichet* would take the creature and give us a colored chit with a number on it. The color of the chit designated the type fowl we had brought. It was sometimes my task to pick up the slaughtered bird in a covered basket and take it home. When I picked up the slaughtered bird, the shoichet would usually give me a candy.

The *shoichet* was a small man with a long beard. He always wore a black hat and a long black kaftan. His house was likewise very small. The windows were so low that even we could look in without straining to gain height. When we looked inside, we noticed that the house was totally ransacked, with the books of his chits and religious books strewn all over the floor. We coveted those little books of bound chits. The small windows of his house were open and we easily stepped into this room of his house. We each picked up a few of the bound chits and quickly left. I don't know what I did with those booklets. Likely I hid them from my parents. I have the sense that I felt some shame about taking them out of his house. It is very likely, that I am the only person left in the world, who remembers the *shoichet* of Humenne.

During one of the deportation actions, my father's younger brother, Miksa (Michael), his wife, and their son, Josef, who was about my age, were deported. My father found out that the transport was heading for Lublin, now in German-occupied Poland. That evening, he took a train to the Slovak-Poland border, following the path of the transport. I don't know the details of what followed, but by ample bribing he found out that his brother was already transported somewhere further into German territories, while his wife and son were still at the Slovak border being held in a transient compound awaiting deportation to Auschwitz. He was able to bribe some of the guards and smuggle Miksa's wife and son out of the compound and bring them back to Humenne. Josef was brought to our house very tired and dirty. My mother gave him a bath and then we, all of us together, ate dinner. But Miksa was gone. My father was devastated by his inability to save his younger brother. For many hours he cried and mourned his brother. In retrospect, I think his sense of failure and grief was perhaps compounded by an event a long time ago. I most likely heard it from Ignac. Miksa stuttered quite severely. When Ignac and Miksa were young, Ignac about nine and Miksa about seven years old, Miksa was sleeping, with his mouth slightly open. As a prank, Ignac sprinkled some baking powder into Miksa's mouth. Someone convinced Ignac that his prank was responsible for Miksa's stuttering. Even though as an adult, Ignac knew that he did not cause his brother's stuttering, the guilt echoed into his adult life.

Throughout the spring of 1942 news came to us that – contrary to what we had been told – those who were deported were not being resettled. They were transported into forced labor camps where they were systematically murdered. Even I, at the age of six, became aware of this. Deportation of Jews continued throughout 1942 and was then abruptly halted on October 20, 1942.

In historical retrospect, several reasons for halting the deportations are now proposed. While the majority of Slovaks were apathetic to or actually supportive of the annihilation of Jews, a small but significant fraction of the population was beginning to actively oppose it. Some of the Slovak Catholic church leaders were in the lead of this opposition. The Vatican finally spoke out firmly against deportation to death camps.[2] Then there were the bribes. The Jewish central organization collected substantial funds that were used to bribe key officials to support the halting of deportation. However, by the time the deportations stopped, 80 percent of Slovak Jewry had been deported in cattle cars to concentration camps in Poland and Germany and murdered. Of the approximately 100,000 Jews who lived in Slovakia pre-WWII, only about 20,000 remained after this first round of deportations.

Even though the deportations stopped, it was evident from the vitriolic pronouncements of the government and local politicians, that our lives in Humenne, and in all of Slovakia, were threatened and in great danger, even for those of us with exemptions. It was only a matter of time before the deportation and annihilation of Slovak Jews would start up again.

How to escape this fate was a continuous subject of adult conversation. Several possibilities were brought up. One was to obtain forged documentation and Arian identity papers. This path was much safer for women than for men because in Slovakia, by and large, only Jewish males were circumcised and therefore the Jewish identity of a male could be very easily revealed. Nevertheless, this was the option my mother and father chose. Another possibility was to prepare a safe hiding place. This had to be done in collaboration with some Gentiles who would be willing to hide a Jewish family. The family could be hidden in some walled-off room or attic in the house of the Gentile, or a safe hiding place could be prepared in the woods, in a bunker-type of dwelling. In either case, the collaborating person would have to bring food to the people in hiding and take away waste. For a plan of this type one had to have complete trust in the Gentile who undertook this task. That person put himself or herself and their families in great danger, because – if caught – they would be deported and most likely killed. My father's two older brothers chose this plan. They initiated arrangements to build a hiding place, really a bunker deep in the mountains, about 30 miles from Humenne.

Another option was – in one way or another – to cross the border into Hungary, where at that time conditions for Jews were far more benign than in Slovakia. Admiral Horthy, a national hero, was named the Regent of Hungary (a king substitute). He became the head of the Hungarian fascist government and formed a reluctant alliance with Hitler's Germany to regain previously lost lands. His government passed restrictive anti-Jewish laws, including restrictions on the professions Jews could practice, prohibitions against intermarriage, and belonging to certain associations. Occasionally, small but murderous pogroms occurred in several areas of Hungary, but Admiral Horthy effectively resisted implementing Hitler's genocidal policies in Hungary. In 1942 and until the beginning of 1944, Jews in Hungary lived relatively peaceful though confined lives without the threat of being deported and murdered. Going to Hungary was a viable option because most Slovak Jews were fluent in Hungarian and often had relatives and friends throughout Hungary. This was the option chosen for me.

6

HUNGARY

The Orphanage

Toward the end of summer 1942, my mother began to receive messages from my paternal grandfather, who lived in Moldava (then in Hungary and called Szepsi), asking to send me to him because he thought I would be safer there with his family than in Slovakia. At the time, it certainly looked that way. These messages were sent in coded letters or via paid gentile messengers who regularly crossed the Hungarian-Slovak border and would deliver the messages either verbally or in writing.

My mother was very hesitant to be separated from me, but all her friends agreed that this was the right thing to do. Everyone who had the means and connections to send their children to Hungary did so. After several of these messages, my mother asked me what I thought we should do. I agreed I should be sent to Hungary. I remember very clearly both her asking me, and my reaction. When I said yes, I was not thinking of safety. I was thinking of the adventure of the train ride and of seeing new places. My mother sent a message to my grandfather telling him that she agreed to send me to live with him, and my grandfather wrote that he would find a reliable person to smuggle me across the border. In retrospect, this was not a very good decision, and my mother was not told about the full extent of the plan.

At the end of September 1942, a tall thin woman came to our house and introduced herself as being sent by my grandfather to take me across the border. She was a Gentile woman who had legal papers to cross the border, while I was to travel as her son. The following morning, my parents and I met the smuggler at the Humenne station. A few minutes later the train arrived and holding my hand, the smuggler and I got on the train. I looked out the window and waved to my parents who were both crying. The train left the station, picking up speed as it hurled through the countryside, stopping in various towns along the way. I don't recall specifically crossing the border, but I imagine it all went smoothly. The train ride was uneventful until we arrived in Košice. I distinctly remember the large sign over the station platform stating the Hungarian name *Kassa*. I was told that my grandfather would be waiting for me, but as we got off the train, I saw no one resembling my grandfather. The smuggler then bent down and whispered to me that there was no one waiting for me. I needed to go to a policeman, and tell him that I was a Jewish boy, and that I was dropped off at the station. I was to say that I don't know who brought me here, and that my parents were killed. I was told to say this all in Slovak, and if anybody asked me whether I had any relatives here in Košice, I must say that I do not know anyone here or anywhere else. She then turned around, walked away, disappearing into the crowd.

The arriving passengers left the platform quickly until there were only a few people remaining, probably waiting for the next train. I looked around and saw two policemen on the station platform talking with each other. I remember this very clearly. Before going up to them I created an image in my mind. I was in a room. Flames were enveloping the walls, ceiling beams were collapsing, and somehow I was saved, but my parents were killed. I went up to the policemen and described to them this scene I had created. I told them that now I was without parents, and that is all that I remember. They asked me my name. Here I had not been coached, so I told them the Hungarian version of my name, with the family name preceding the given name: Davidovits Pal. The policemen put me in their car and drove to me to the police station. We walked up a set of stairs and they opened the door to a small room with a table and a chair. They told me to sit and wait. After a while a man, in civilian clothing, came to question me. He asked my name again, and asked very explicitly whether I had any relatives in Košice. In fact, my aunt Erzsi, that is my mother's youngest sister, and my uncle Ernest (Ernő), lived in Košice, but I firmly adhered to my story, as the smuggler had instructed me. "I am an orphan and know no one here." The interrogator stated, "You are a Jew, yes?" and I said that I was. I also told him that I was getting very hungry and asked if I could get something to eat. The interrogator said, "No, no eating here." He then left and I was kept in that small room for what seemed a very long time. The room had a small window through which I could see a courtyard. Outside it was getting dark, and I was getting more and more hungry.

Finally, the door opened and a young man walked in. He told me his name. I don't remember it exactly, but I think it sounded like "Zacharias", so that is what I will call him here. "I heard you were hungry", he said, and I nodded my head. "You will come with me, and I will find something for you to eat." We walked out the door and a policeman handed me my small suitcase. Outside the police station we got on a streetcar, which was very exciting, because I do not remember ever having ridden on a streetcar before. We traveled for a while before we got off in front of a yellow building on a street that I subsequently learned was called *Harang Utza*, the bell street. The street was dark, quiet and deserted. We walked through an arched entrance into a courtyard surrounded by several buildings. Zacharias led me into one of these buildings and through a large door into a long room with two rows of tables and chairs. "This is the dining room. We have many children living with us and I think you will like it here. But now the children have eaten and have already gone to sleep. I'll just go into the kitchen to see what is there for you to eat." He came back soon with a large pot filled with peeled boiled potatoes and a smaller bowl with raw garlic cloves. I ate several boiled potatoes and way too many raw garlic cloves. My hunger was satiated, but I felt a little sick. To this day the odor of raw garlic makes me a bit queasy.

After I ate, Zacharias took me out into the dark courtyard and then into another of the larger buildings. That building had a foyer with several doors opening from it. Zacharias opened one of the doors and turned on the light. In the long narrow room there were two rows of metal beds, about 20 beds in a row, with a space between each bed barely adequate for a person to squeeze through. Most of the beds were occupied by boys about my age, lying down. As soon as the light was turned on, the boys sat up, and leaning on their elbows they stared at me. Zacharias said loudly "This is Pali, he is the new member of our group." He led me to one of the few empty beds, with a pillow and blanket on it, and instructed me to keep my suitcase under the bed. I quickly pulled off my shoes, took off my trousers and laid down. Zacharias turned off the light and left.

I was in the orphanage for about five months and from that time, all I can summon up are two more memories. One of a day away from the orphanage, when a group of women, I should say ladies, because they were all dressed in elegant clothing and wore fancy hats, fetched some of us. This must have been an event something like "take an orphan home for a day". One of the women took me by carriage to her apartment which was in a large building. The apartment ceiling was very high and the windows were large overlooking a street with streetcar tracks in the middle. An old woman sat on a chair by a table, an open book in front of her. She was silent, while her fingers moved rapidly across the page and I realized that she was blind. My host introduced the woman as her mother. She beckoned me over, and then slowly touched my eyes, nose, mouth and ears, and said in Hungarian, "What a beautiful little boy."

A maid came in and set the table with milk and cookies and some other foods which I don't remember. While I was eating, my host paced back and forth in the room. Finally, she sat down on the sofa and my host, her mother and I, sat quietly until my host got off the sofa, handed me a little bag and said that in it were cookies for me to eat later. She then took me back to the orphanage.

My other memory is that of leaving the orphanage. One morning, Zacharias approached me, with my suitcase in his hand, gave it to me and said that my grandfather had come to take me to his home. He led me to the courtyard where my grandfather stood waiting. I ran up to him, he hugged me, and we walked out through the courtyard to the street.

As I am tugging at my memories I realize that none of them are actually from the orphanage itself. They are from my coming, being away for a day, and leaving. The actual months in the orphanage are a total blank in my memory. Perhaps the total sense of abandonment blanked out my thoughts and feelings.

Later I found out why I was left isolated in that orphanage for so long. My grandfather was a very cautious man. He wanted my coming to live with him to be completely legal and so he sought full documentation that I was an orphan with no relations in Košice. When he finally came to get me, he was my legally appointed guardian. This took some bribing and some time, but he had eventually accomplished it. Meanwhile, my mother thought that I was living with him all along. She was regularly receiving letters from my grandparents describing my fictional life with them, and had no idea that I was in an orphanage. My aunt Erzsi and uncle Ernő knew, and cooperated with my grandfather's fiction.

In 1942 and in 1943 many parents in Slovakia had their children smuggled into Hungary, just as I was. It seemed the surest way to save them from deportation and death, and many of them ended up in Košice, where the resources to house and take care of them were soon exhausted. Responding to the situation, two Jewish women set up and organized a Jewish orphanage in Košice. They collected money, rented buildings, obtained the required permits and supervised the orphanage operation. In an interesting coincidence, after the war, one of these women, Klara, became, in effect, my aunt, when my uncle Ernő married Klara's sister Eva. Klara was a woman with a great sense of responsibility, abilities, commitment, and moral strength.

Klara

During the spring of 1944, most of the Jewish population of Košice and the towns surrounding it, men, women and children were herded onto the grounds of the brick factory at the outskirts of Košice, from where they were deported to Auschwitz. The brick factory was particularly well suited for this purpose because railroad tracks built to bring in raw material and ship out bricks led directly to the factory. The conditions at the brick factory were extremely bad; lack of sanitary facilities, and no adequate shelter. The shortage of food was especially severe. Klara collected funds and organized several soup kitchens that prepared more than 10,000 meals a day. When the freight cars arrived and the deportation began, Klara accompanied the 52 children that were in the orphanage to Auschwitz, comforting them as much as anyone could be comforted in those horrible times. At Auschwitz, in a process called *Selektion*, children and the elderly were separated from those deemed able to work, and were herded directly into the gas chambers, to be killed immediately. Those selected for work were stripped of their clothing and possessions, were issued striped prisoner clothing, and assigned to barracks.

Klara, together with her two young nieces Helen and Oli, were housed in barracks with about 40 other women. The conditions were awful: hard labor, lack of food, often spoiled food, horrible sanitation facilities, and frequent illnesses. Most of the Jews in Auschwitz died or were killed. Klara and her two nieces, though close to death, survived until the Russian army liberated the camp on January 27, 1945.

When Klara returned to Košice, she discovered the horrible reality. Her husband and two teenage sons, aged 13 and 17, had been killed. The pictures of those two handsome young men were on the wall of Klara's apartment for 50 years till she died, looking out at the world they were not given a chance to see. Such a wound to a mother can never be healed. But Klara's heart never hardened. It opened even wider to the world. She married Eugene Weinberger, a man whom my family knew from Humenne. So many members of our families had been killed in the Holocaust that the survivors all sought new family connections. It was around this time that Klara became in effect my aunt, when my uncle Ernest, whose wife and son were also killed in Auschwitz, married Klara's younger sister Eva.

Shortly after the war, Klara and Eva, with their new husbands, immigrated to Canada to join their brother, Charles, and sister-in-law, Freida, in Toronto. My mother, stepfather and I joined them in Toronto in 1949. Around the same time, Helen and Oli, Klara and Eva's nieces, moved to Canada as well. Although I left Toronto for New York in 1958, I returned several times a year to Toronto to visit the family, including Helen and Oli, who were now married, each with two children. Both Helen and Oli talked frequently about their time in Auschwitz, and they attributed their survival and the survival of several other women in their barracks to Klara's selfless efforts. In the evenings, when the lights were out in the barracks, she sought out the most despondent women and talked to them in subdued whispers, perhaps giving them some hope. She often gave away her meager food allotment to someone near starvation, saying that she could afford to lose weight. At the beginning of her interment at Auschwitz, Klara was a hefty woman, but by the time of liberation, she was as emaciated as the other survivors.

Helen wrote a memoir about her year in Auschwitz which she gave me to read. Here she described an event that occurred in the early fall of 1944. Klara was suffering from severe diarrhea. In the middle of the night, she had to get up to go to the latrine some hundred yards from the barracks. The latrine consisted of a long sewage channel covered by stone slabs, each with a hole in its center, to seat the user. Klara was alone in the latrine at this late hour, and she sat on one of the slabs, centering herself over its hole. It appears that the slab was cracked and as Klara tried to center herself, it broke in half and slipped out of position and Klara fell into the sewage channel, filled with feces and urine. There was no way that she could climb out of this slippery miasma without someone's aid. She called for help, which was in itself dangerous, because the SS guard who would come was as likely as not to shoot a prisoner in such a predicament. This time however, the guard who came behaved unexpectedly. He removed the broken stone slab and extended the barrel of his rifle to Klara. He told Klara to hold on tightly and with his help she climbed out of the sewage. He told her to wait, and a few minutes later he returned with a few dirty rags. "This is the best I can do", he said and walked away. Klara wiped herself off as best as she could and staggered back to the barracks. It was clear that the stench followed her, so she sat down on the outside stairs and waited for dawn.

The prisoners were woken at 4 am and had to come out immediately for the roll call. When the women came out they saw Klara sitting outside, totally dejected. A few of the women helped her up and propping her up as best as they could, they lined up for roll call. Immediately after roll call the women lined up with their tin cups to receive their only warm liquid of the day, about 12 ounces of ersatz chicory coffee. They then had a few minutes in their barracks before they had to line up again to be marched to their work detail.

Without any discussion, someone appeared in the barracks with two pails into which the women poured their cups of ersatz coffee. With this warm liquid they washed and cleaned Klara, brought her some dry clothing and got her ready for another day.

The early years of my family's life in Canada were not easy. In their middle age now, the adults had to build new lives; and they did that; filled with family, love and friendships. As soon as Klara had any free time she started again to work for others wherever she saw the need. In just one of her several activities, she organized the distribution of *pushkes*, a tin container for collecting coins dedicated to a variety of causes. These *pushkes*, which she periodically picked up, yielded many thousands of dollars each year, for more than 30 years during her performance of this task.

In the presence of Klara I always had a sense of spaciousness, a wonderful sense of being welcomed with joy. In her last years, Klara was very often in pain, and spent her time indoors in her apartment. Here she was most comfortable, and lovingly cared for by her family and friends. But even in these last years I never had the sense that the pain has constricted her world. Klara's joy at seeing me was always there.

In one of my last visits with Klara, she said to me, "My dearest Paul, I have so much time to think and I often think about all the wonders of the world. How did it all come to be? Look at just one species, the parrots. Do you know how many different kinds there are? What beautiful feathers they have? And all those parrots know exactly what to do, how to be in this world?" And that is the way also Klara was in the world. She always knew just how to be.

Moldava

My memories resumed almost immediately after my grandfather took me out of the orphanage. I must have looked rather shabby because right from the orphanage, my grandfather brought me to a barber for a haircut and then to a clothing store where he bought me a whole new outfit. I changed into my new clothing and we went by taxi to my aunt Erzsi's house where she lived with her husband Geza and my cousin Evi. We then went to a well-known photographer Gyori and Boros, where they took a picture of my cousin Evi and me, which was mailed to my mother as proof of my wellbeing. That is how this picture found its way into my mother's album.

My cousin Evi and me.

That evening we took the train to Moldava, a short train ride from Košice. I was warmly welcomed and hugged by my grandmother and other relatives that were waiting for me. I must have been quite disturbed when I first arrived from the orphanage. For several weeks I urinated in my bed almost every night, waking up with the sheets soaked. I was greatly embarrassed by this, but no one ever mentioned my bed wetting. The following evening I found the bedding changed and the bed dry as if nothing had happened. Early on I would also often wake up in the middle of the night greatly frightened. I would call out and my grandmother would come, sit near my bed, hold my hand and talk to me softly till I fell back asleep.

After a few weeks with my grandparents I began to fall into the routine of the household. My grandparents' house did not have central heating. The bedrooms and the living room had stoves with floor to ceiling tiles. The stove tiles in my bedroom were shiny green with interspersed triangular patterns. As I remember it, my grandparents employed two maids who did a variety of cleaning, housekeeping and cooking chores. After I put myself to bed, one of the maids would come into my bedroom with a pail full of coal. She opened the stove door and filled the stove with fuel, then securely closed the door, said good night and left the room. My grandmother would then come in, most of the time alone, occasionally with my grandfather. She would kiss me on the forehead, wish me peaceful sleep, turn off the light, and leave. In the morning the house was usually awakened by the maids who went from room to room rekindling the stove fires. The house was always comfortably warm, even on the coldest days.

During the mid-1800s, as the Enlightenment began to spread through western and central Europe, increasing number of Jews moved away from strict Orthodoxy and formed separate factions that in Hungarian lands were called Neolog and Status Quo. Each group had its own synagogues and rabbis. In many larger cities these factions split further into sub-groups with separately evolving customs and rituals. As in the large cities, Jews in Moldava also spanned the spectrum of commitment to traditional Judaism. However, Moldava, a small town with a relatively small Jewish population, had only one synagogue with one rabbi who served all the Jews in the community. Most Jews of Moldava adhered to traditional Orthodox customs and traditions, but many only in public. My grandparents' home was strictly kosher and my grandfather attended synagogue every Friday and Saturday. At home however, I have never seen him wear a skull cap or put on phylacteries or recite privately the morning or afternoon prayers.

As in any Orthodox home, on Friday afternoons the kitchen was humming with my grandmother and the household preparing the Shabbat meals. The main Shabbat meal served Saturday early afternoon was *cholent*. Meat, vegetables, and a variety of spices were placed in a large pot, covered by wax paper which tied down around the rim of the pot. On the wax paper my grandmother wrote our name. Friday evening before Shabbat my grandfather and I went to the synagogue and I pulled the small wagon with the pot of cholent on it. On the way to the synagogue we left the wagon with the pot in the back yard of the baker. Most of the Jewish families did the same thing. The baker placed the pots in the pre-heated oven where the cholent cooked slowly all night. We picked up the cooked cholent Saturday after the morning services. I remember that the family names on the cold wax paper were only faintly visible, but after baking, the wax paper became brittle and the family names stood out prominently. The atmosphere was warm and friendly as people picked out their pot of cholent. People wished each other *Git Shabbes* and I pulled the wagon with the cholent back home.

When we got home, a short walk from the baker, the table was already set with plates and silverware, *Challah* and the other part of the Shabbat meal, a big plate of *Ayer mit tzvibel*. Although in my grandparents' home Yiddish was not spoken, some of the food was always referred to by its Yiddish name. *Ayer mit tzvibel* consisted of mashed hard-boiled eggs and fried cut-up onions. After the afternoon Shabbat meal the adults went off to take a nap for a couple of hours.

Once a month or so a goose was bought at the market and brought home to be fattened by force feeding. The force feeding was no longer done by my grandmother. One of the maids did the work. After about two weeks of force feeding the goose was slaughtered by the *shoichet*, its esophagus was removed, and it was then my task to take the esophagus to the rabbi for examination. The rabbi would blow up the esophagus, trans-illuminate it with a candle, look for blemishes or injuries caused by the force feeding. He would then decide whether the goose was kosher or not. Once I returned home with the message from the rabbi that the esophagus showed the goose not to be kosher. My grandmother grumbled, "If this goose had belonged to.." and here she mentioned the name of our neighbor much poorer that we were. "The Rabbi would have pronounced the goose kosher." Still, she adhered to the Rabbi's decision and gave the goose away to a Gentile neighbor.

I asked Gedaliah Fleer, a rabbi in Jerusalem, how this examination is related to *kashrut*. He explained that this is of concern when the bird is force fed. Force feeding itself does not make the goose un-kosher. However, during the two or three weeks of force feeding, the esophagus may be injured. Other organ injuries may be caused by the mass of the liver, that during force feeding increases by as much as a factor of ten. Such organ injuries, if observed would also make the animal un-kosher.

I lived with my grandparents in Moldava from the spring of 1943 to the spring of 1944. Life during that year was peaceful with occasional visits to Košice to see my relatives, the families of Ernő and Erzsi.

In the late summer of 1943, we traveled by train for several hours to Huszt to visit the family of my grandparents' daughter, my aunt Ilona. As mentioned earlier, I am not certain about her name. She was married to a man named Ludwig (Lajcsi in Hungarian) Korach. He was a prosperous pharmacist, who owned one of the three pharmacies in Huszt. The visit to Huszt was an annual event lasting two to three weeks.

Huszt is on the border of Ukraine in a region called Subcarpathian Russia. In 1943, this region was controlled by Hungary, but over the years the town was part of Czechoslovakia, Ukraine, Poland, and briefly it was an independent state. As a result, the name of the town has several alternate spellings. At the time of our visit, the town was part of Hungary. When we visited Huszt, the town had a population of about 10,000, a third of which was Jewish. As in most central European communities, Jews ranged from highly assimilated to ultra-Orthodox chasidim. At that time all three pharmacists as well as the seven doctors in Huszt were Jews. These professionals formed the social circle of my Huszt relatives.

We arrived in Huszt in the late afternoon and my uncle, Korach Lajcsi, was waiting for us in his car and drove us to his house. Huszt, as I remember it, was a mixture of a city and a backward village. The Korach house was large and actually seemed more modern than our house in Moldava. For one, it had running water and an indoor toilet. After we arrived and my grandparents unpacked, I was given permission to go outside and explore the neighborhood.

The Korach house was on a paved main street with a row of houses and several stores. Behind the house was a path overgrown with grass. I walked along the path that led to a large unpainted barn. I peeked in and saw a man brushing a chestnut brown horse. The man was wearing pants made of thick white cloth commonly worn by peasants in Ruthenia and also in Slovakia. I had never seen a horse being brushed, so I asked the man in Hungarian why he was doing that. He answered in Ruthenian, which is very close to Slovak so I understood his answer. He explained that the horse has been working and now has to be brushed to make sure that his hair is smooth because brushing keeps the horse clean by getting the bugs out. This was his horse, that he used to do all sorts of work, and he wanted to make sure it remained healthy. Then he asked if I was part of the family that was visiting the Korachs. I said yes. He turned away from his horse and looked at me more closely. He noticed that I had a wart under my nose between my two nostrils. That wart had been there for a long time and often I absentmindedly picked at it which made the wart hurt. He bent down looked at the wart and asked if I would like to have the wart removed. Emphatically I said yes. He plucked one hair out of the horse's tail and kneeled down, tying the horsehair tightly around the wart. Then, he cut off the edges of the horse hair with a sharp knife. The man said the wart would fall off in two or three days.

I must have looked funny with the string under my nose because the three Korach boys, Otto, Laci and Gyuri, laughed at me when I got back to the house. I looked into a mirror and I did look funny. The wart under my nose with the two ends of the horsehair sticking out looked like a little brown mustache. When my grandfather saw me he simply said, "This may work." And it did. In three days, the wart, together with the horsehair, fell off. The wart never reappeared.

I already mentioned my three Korach cousins, but now I really liked them. They were all several years older than I was. At this point I was seven and a half years old and I think they were about 13, 12, and 10. They were my heroes. They could do everything better than I could. One hot afternoon the four of us went to the edge of town to the river that flowed through Huszt. I think it may have been the Tisza river. The shores of the river were deserted. We walked some distance into the woods away from the shore where they showed me a raft they were building in secret. The raft, they told me, was now completed. It consisted of a bunch of planks and logs tied together with rope. We dragged the raft to the river, pushed it into the water and all four of us climbed onto it. The river here was swift, deep, and fairly wide. After a few minutes of an exciting ride, the raft hit a boulder and started to fall apart. Logs began to loosen and come off, one after the other.

My cousins knew how to swim, but I didn't. So as the logs peeled away, I held on to the last log and they pushed me to a little island a few yards in diameter near the shore of the river. Here they could touch the bottom, but it was too deep for me. They helped me get to the shore and swore me to secrecy about our misadventure. I kept the secret.

After a few weeks in Huszt, we returned by train to Moldava. It was still summer and shortly after we returned, I remember an afternoon when, in the care of one of the two young maids who served in our house, we went swimming in the Bodva river. A crowd of young people male and female was in the water playing in a swimming hole under a small waterfall. The water was not very deep; only up to the chests of the people in the water. The girl in charge of my safety let go of my hand and dashed into the crowd screeching and splashing. While the water was only chest high for the people in the swimming hole, it was over my head, and I began to sink screaming and trashing. But my screams just merged with the joyous noise of the crowd and no one paid any attention to my distress. I sank, began to swallow and inhale water. Finally, someone noticed my loosing struggle and pulled me up onto the shore. I coughed and vomited but recovered quickly. Once again, I was made to promise that I would keep this near-drowning a secret.

We returned from Huszt to Moldava toward the end of August 1943. I have an approximate awareness of the date because shortly after we returned, I started to prepare for the start of the school year. We went to Košice to get me some new fall clothing and a satchel for my school supplies. I was three month short of my eighth birthday and I was entering grade two of the Moldava public school.

In the morning and early afternoon I attended public school, while I was enrolled in Hebrew school during the afternoon. The curriculum consisted of memorizing the Hebrew Torah and its translation into Yiddish. The drill was one line of Hebrew followed by its Yiddish equivalent. This was all done in a traditional chant that I still remember. The main problem with this teaching method was that we boys understood neither Hebrew nor Yiddish. I imagine that had we kept this up, eventually would have learned both Yiddish and the Torah.

At this time, in spite of a host of anti-Jewish laws, Jews in Hungary were allowed to live relatively peacefully. But unknown to us, our world was about to change drastically.

7

OUT OF HUNGARY

For the German armies the situation on the battlefield was deteriorating rapidly. In February 1943, the German army and its Hungarian, Italian and Romanian allies were defeated in Stalingrad. The total Axis casualties (Germans, Romanians, Italians, and Hungarians) are estimated to be more than 800,000 dead, wounded, missing, or captured. Hungarian casualties were about 140,000. This defeat initiated the non-stop retreat of the German armies till their total defeat in 1945.

In the spring of 1944, the Russian army was coming closer to the borders of Hungary and it became evident to most people that Germany was going to lose the war. The government of Miklós Horthy began secret negotiations with the allies for armistice and a separate peace. When Hitler found out about the possible breakaway of Hungary, he ordered the invasion of Hungary. German troops entered Hungary on March 19, 1944. The Germans deposed Horthy, put him under house arrest and installed a new government led by the leaders of the fascist and virulently antisemitic Arrow Cross party. Up until that point, Horthy's Hungarian government had resisted the killing of Hungarian Jews. Now a central goal of the Germans and the new Hungarian government was the total destruction of the Hungarian Jews. Adolf Eichmann was in charge of organizing the killing of Hungarian Jewry.

We in Moldava had not yet seen any German soldiers but we were all keenly aware of the dangerous change in our situation. I remember clearly the Friday after the German army entered Hungary. My grandfather and I were on our way to synagogue when we came across a small group surrounding two young men in full Chasidic garb, long black coats, fur hats, talking excitedly. They had just returned from Košice where they saw German soldiers marching on the street and walking on the sidewalks. They ignored the two Moldava chasidim and did not harm them in any way. The two young men meant to reassure us that we were in no danger.

Overt antisemitism was now on the rise. Mr. Balog, my grade two teacher was a virulent antisemite, a member of the local branch of the Iron Cross. He had jet-black hair, smoothed flat back, with a part in the middle. One morning, soon after the Germans entered Hungary, he began the class with a story. He started by saying, "A huge flock of black crows descended on our beautiful country, on our beautiful Hungary. These crows ate up all the fruits and produce of our country." He continued in this mode for several minutes and then he pointed at me and at the other Jewish children in the class and he shouted. "These crows are the Jews, but we will take care of this problem." This was pretty scary.

We were expected to come to school a few minutes early and play in the school yard before a bell summoned us to the classrooms. The next morning, I was playing a ball game at one end of the school yard when I saw Balog's son, who was in my class, shoving my little cousin Marika, Zoli's daughter, and calling her a filthy Jew. He tripped her and pushed her to the ground.

I became enraged; I ran toward him, hit him as hard as I could and threw him to the ground. The teacher supervising the playground pulled me off him. After a while, the bell rang and we all entered the classrooms. Little Balog did not come to class. The teacher, Balog, started his class by saying, "This morning, Pali (he pointed at me), attacked my son. He hit my son very hard but I am happy about that. This will make my son hate Jews even more." At that point I stood up and said "Mr. Balog, if you're so happy that I beat up your son, I'll gladly beat him up again." I don't know why I said that. Perhaps to spite him, or to anger him. Maybe I actually thought that he would be pleased with my offer; but that is what I said. Balog jumped up from his seat at the table in front of the class, grabbed me by my jacket and slammed me against the wall. He then opened the classroom door and threw me violently out of the class into the hall. I went home and told my grandfather what had happened. I think he went to school and spoke to the principal. The next day I was back in class as was Balog's son. I can't retrieve any memories about classroom life after that.

Passover 1944

In 1944 the first *seder* fell on Friday April 7, and Jewish life in Moldava continued normally till then. Preparations for this important holiday were in full swing. The community organized baking of *matzot*. This was done in a hut in the back yard of the synagogue. An oven was set up, and each family signed up for a specific time to come and witness their *matzah* being baked. This was a highly controlled process. Small batches of flour were mixed with water and quickly kneaded. Within 18 minutes of combining water with the flour, the dough had to be inserted into the heated oven to prevent the dough from starting to leaven.

For weeks I had been preparing for Passover. We were going to have a big family *seder* and because I was the youngest child who could read, it was my task to chant the traditional four questions. My grandfather helped me memorize the questions with the cantillation and then tested me until he was satisfied that I was doing it perfectly. I still remember this traditional Ashkenazi cantillation and during our family *seders* we now sing it together.

Shortly before Passover my grandfather decided to go to Košice to buy some shirts for himself and for me. I accompanied him. That trip brought about a reprimand from a neighbor who lived a few houses up the street from us and whose name or face I no longer recall but his reprimand has stayed with me to this day. We entered a small clothing store near the center of town. Grandfather introduced me to the storekeeper. Clearly, they knew each other and talked for a while. When we were ready to leave the storekeeper bent to my height and said, "Your neighbor is an old friend of mine. I have not seen him for a while. Would you please tell him that I send my regards and that I think of him. Would you do that?" I said I would.

A week or so later, my grandfather and I met the neighbor on a Friday evening on our way to the synagogue. My grandfather stopped and talked to the neighbor for a while and then, as we were parting, the neighbor pulled me aside and told me that he spoke to his friend the shopkeeper in Košice and that I had not kept my promise to transmit his friend's greetings. In a quiet voice he told me how important it is to transmit greetings and messages. The message one carries could be the last living connection between two people and the messenger must make sure that the connection is completed. I have never forgotten that. A few months later both men were killed in Auschwitz.

April 7th arrived and the whole family was preparing for the first *seder*. In the morning, the complete set of Passover dishes and silverware, used only for the eight days of Passover, were taken out of storage. The holiday table, a large long table in the living room, was set with a white table cloth and all of the Passover dishes including the ceremonial plate were set on the table. But the *seder* was not held that night. A policeman who was a friend of our family came to warn us. That evening we would be forced to leave our home and the following day deported to a ghetto set up in Košice.

My grandfather collected the family jewels, gold necklaces and bracelets, diamond engagement rings, gold watches and broches, put these items in a shoebox and wrapped the box in wax paper. He went to the shed in the garden where firewood and garden tools were kept and – as he later told me – buried the box under a pile of logs.

A police detachment came in the late afternoon and told us that a truck would pick us up in a short while to take us to a central collecting place for deportation. We were allowed to take with us a small suitcase each, and every family a container of food. The only food ready to be taken with us was *matza* and the hard-boiled eggs.

The overall deportation was organized by Eichmann. Jews from smaller communities would be collected and shipped to larger cities, from where the combined Jewish population would be transported to Auschwitz. Eichmann's choice to begin the process on Passover was of course not a coincidence. It was meant to mock the exodus from Egypt.

We packed in a big rush and were ready just as the flatbed truck arrived. I remember that it was getting dark. Some people were already on the back of the truck when my grandfather, grandmother, uncle Zoli, his wife and two children, and I climbed on. I am not certain of the location for the central collection of the Moldava Jews. I remember it as the basement of the synagogue. A second cousin, five years older than I, remembers the place as the auditorium of the high school. There may have been more than one place where they gathered us.

When we got to the collection hall, many people, some of whom I knew, were already there, sitting on the floor huddled in family groups. Moldava was a town of about 2,000 people, of whom 500 were Jews, so it was a large crowd collected in the hall. People were scared and crying. Of course, people were also hungry, because nobody had had time to sit down and eat the Passover dinner. Most people brought the same *seder* food along. Each family spread out some sort of a blanket on the floor and we began to eat our hard-boiled eggs with the dry *matza*.

I still remember the family next to us. I don't know who they were. They had brought a big pot filled with eggs but they had not boiled them long enough. As they cracked the eggs open they found a watery mess. My grandmother took some of our hard-boiled eggs and gave them to that family. As I remember it, a few other people brought over some of their eggs as well.

And then, in the midst of the crying and the noise and the confusion, the rabbi stood up and started to chant a prayer.

It may have been *el mol el rachamim*, the prayer for the dead. The people in the synagogue quieted down. The panic and the fear seem to have subsided and some degree of calmness set in. I don't remember much about the rest of the night, I probably slept some.

Very early the following morning we were taken out onto the street by the police and lined up. We were marched in a long line to the train station which was about half a mile outside the town. The street was lined by the non-Jewish population of Moldava. Many were jeering, shouting obscene words and spitting at us. Others were just silent. At the railroad station a train of cattle cars was waiting for us. We were herded into the cattle cars, the doors were slammed shut and locked. Then the train started off for Košice which was about an hour away. It was a slow train ride.

The Ghetto

Once the freight train arrived in Košice, we were marched to the old Jewish section of the town. The Jews who had lived there had already been deported to the brick factory that served as a holding area until the final deportation to Auschwitz. We were assigned to an empty apartment with three other families. The ghetto was surrounded by barbed wire, prepared for our arrival. The entrances and exits were guarded by German soldiers and Hungarian police. There were, as I now remember, some Gentiles living in this area as well, who had not been evicted. They could go in and out of the ghetto by showing their identity cards.

Meanwhile in Humenne, my parents had found out what was happening to Hungarian Jews and specifically where my grandparents and I were. They were frantic. During the period of about three weeks that we stayed in the ghetto, they sent two or three smugglers, that I was aware of, to get me out, but my grandfather would not let me go. I was registered as part of his family and I suppose he was worried what would happen if the authorities checked and found that I was missing.

Smuggled out

Then early one morning, flatbed trucks drove into the ghetto, and Jews, house by house, were herded by Iron Cross troops into the streets and onto these trucks, for transportation to the edge of the town to a staging center which, I later found out, was the brick factory, where the out-of-town Jews joined the Košice Jews, for transport to Auschwitz.

By that time, all illusions about a future for us Jews had vanished. Coincidentally, that morning, another smuggler sent by my parents arrived. I didn't see him. He sent a message into the ghetto to my grandfather that this was the last chance to let me go.

This time my grandfather agreed and he took me aside. We stood next to a large window. I could see the street through the window. Outside the trucks were already being loaded and people who were not moving fast enough were being pushed on. I still remember clearly looking up at my grandfather. He put his hands on my shoulders, and told me that I was going back to my parents. He said that the person who was taking me back was waiting for me outside the ghetto sitting on a bench in the adjacent park. He described the man but I no longer remember his description. First, I had to get out of the ghetto. My grandfather told me to take my ball and pretend that I was playing with it. That way maybe I could get through the gate guarded by the police. I remember as the two of us stood there, my grandfather towering over me asked two things of me. He said, "Don't change your name. Keep the family name." He continued, "Tell your mother as soon as you see her that the jewels were buried in the woodshed under the woodpile."

I then went downstairs, left the apartment and walked toward the street which was the exit from the ghetto. I pretended to play with the ball, and walked right past the two guards. I then walked to the small park near the ghetto and there sitting on a bench was a man who, I was told by my grandfather, would smuggle me out of Hungary back to my parents.

I don't remember exactly how we got to the border. I do remember a train ride to a small village and then a long hike trekking through a forest, occasionally on a narrow path covered by slippery leaves. Along the way a second man joined us. He and the smuggler were friends and he brought us some bread and bacon. After walking for what seemed a very long time, I developed a blister on the back of my right foot. I told this to the smuggler. Our new companion directed me to take off my shoe and sock and to sit on a log. I did as he told me. And this I still remember with clarity and continued amazement. The smuggler's friend, a tall man standing over me, covered one nostril and from the other nostril he blew a big booger of snot that landed exactly on my blister. He told me to put back my sock and shoe and we continued walking. The pain of the blister almost completely disappeared.

After several hours of walking we reached our goal, the edge of the forest. At this point it was beginning to get dark. In front of us was a large meadow, and beyond it some more trees. I heard faintly the barking of dogs. The smuggler told me that behind those trees was a small river that marked the border. He would now go and see if we could get across the border at his usual place of crossing. He told me to wait quietly at the edge of the forest behind some bushes.

So I waited at the edge of the forest. In front of me was a meadow and then the imagined river which was the border. The smuggler came back a few minutes later, alone, and told me that we could not cross where he thought we would because it was too heavily guarded. I should stay and wait for him where I was. He would find another place to cross. His friend, he said, went home. He could handle the crossing alone. So I waited sitting behind a bush. Dusk turned to darkness. Behind me was the dark forest and in front of me the meadow. I heard the howling of dogs, sometimes louder, sometimes quieter. I realized that these were guard dogs of the border patrols. I sat there alone, most of the night. I remember thinking what might happen to me if the smuggler did not return, but I don't remember being afraid at all.

Dawn was breaking and the smuggler still did not return. I was now worried that I would be abandoned here. I had no idea what to do, so I just continued to wait. After some time, the smuggler returned, walking out of the woods behind me. He found a place where we could cross. We walked some distance along the edge of the woods and then down to the river. The river was only a few meters wide and shallow. We took off our shoes and socks and with the smuggler holding my hand we quickly crossed into Slovakia.

After some more walking, this time along a worn path, we reached a farmhouse. It was now late afternoon and I was cold, tired and hungry. In the kitchen of the farmhouse a man and a woman sat at a table eating. They were friends or relatives of the smuggler because as soon as we walked in they jumped up from the table and hugged and kissed him. They gave me some food and told me to warm up and get some sleep. I slept on top of the oven which was not an uncommon arrangement in peasant houses. Part of the brick oven near the chimney remained warm from the day's use and was a good place to sleep on cold nights.

In the morning, the smuggler took me to the train station near the village, and there was my father Ignac waiting for me. When he saw me he scooped me up in his arms and he hugged me and cried. We then traveled by train to Humenne. We got off the train and walked to the corso, a long boulevard reaching out from the train station and running through the town. Some distance down the boulevard was my dog Pityu, my mother and her sister-in-law Bozsi. Pityu was the first to notice me. He ran full speed toward me and leaped into my arms. My mother followed Pityu, running towards me. The first thing I told her, lest I forget, was where my grandfather buried the jewels. I was back home again.

Aftermath

In the mid-1980s when I was about 50 years old, I developed a backache in the cervical region. This was certainly a notable pain but did not explain the intensity of my response. Gradually, I became severely depressed, and as time went on I began to suffer with intense insomnia – but not just insomnia. I would wake up in the middle of the night around 2 am and fear would take over. This was a palpable physical sensation of intense fear that gradually spread throughout my body. The fear usually started at the pit of my stomach. Then it spread down my thighs, my feet, then up my spine. The fear then circulated through my body like a malevolent snake. It is difficult to describe or explain how fear can be felt in one's arm, leg or torso, or the body as a whole, but there I was, in full horror, night after night. For hours I lay alone in bed – gripped, immersed in this fear – until dawn came and I would get up and proceed with my daily tasks as best as I could.

This went on with growing intensity for about six months. Then one night in the middle of being gripped by fear, a small window opened up and a question presented itself. Why was I so afraid? Yes, I had a backache but this was not paralyzing pain. My life was not threatened. My family and my job were safe. So where did this overwhelming paralyzing fear come from? And then my thoughts flashed to that time when I was smuggled across the border from Hungary to Slovakia. I saw myself – a little boy totally alone – hiding behind a bush in the dark, with dogs howling, not knowing whether I would be abandoned, or whether that stranger, the smuggler, would return. And yet, I clearly remember that crouched and hiding there, I did not feel any fear. I just waited.

Lying in bed in the middle of the night, the realization came to me that I must have been petrified. But somehow, I blocked that fear. Was it the fear of that little boy that I now felt? Was that fear somehow locked in my body and now that my life seemed quite safe, triggered by the backache, that terror was released and manifested itself? I don't know whether this is a fantasy I created, or a psycho-physiological fact, but it gave me some comfort and some relief from the nightly terror visitations. At night, I began to repeat the process of imagining myself in the woods as a little boy and feeling that fear. I imagined what I must have felt during the dark cold night hearing the nearby river and the barking dogs. Gradually as that image came back more clearly and assumed a stronger reality, the intense fear that I, in my adult years, experienced night after night, began to subside as did my backache. Gradually, after some months, my life resumed its customary feeling of normalcy.

8

ON THE RUN

I was now back with my parents, and in a few days life seemed to have returned to normal. I slept in my own bed, played with my dog and my cousins, and ate familiar meals cooked by my mother. I was not enrolled in school yet because after speaking only Hungarian for more than a year, I had to regain fluency in Slovak.

However, my peaceful life in Humenne did not last long, and going back to school became very soon a moot question. The armies of the Soviet Union were moving rapidly west toward Slovakia. It was now clear to most people that Germany was going to lose the war. The German government and the Slovak fascist party were once again totally focused on the complete annihilation of the Jews of Slovakia. Tiso, the president of fascist Slovakia, was under pressure to resume the deportation of Jews to concentration camps outside the borders of Slovakia. It was now public knowledge that these camps were constructed for the principal purpose of murdering Jews, although a large number of Roma (Gypsies) were also killed. Tiso however, as an ordained priest, was also under the opposing pressure, mainly from the Vatican, not to participate openly in such murderous activities. As a compromise, his government delayed deportation by ordering all Jews from eastern Slovakia to resettle by May 15, 1944 in the western part of the country. We all knew that this was the last step in the final deportation and annihilation of all Jews of Slovakia. We had to arrange as best as we could to escape from this fate.

I already described the frantic activities the night before our departure; the preparation of the false identity documents, the arrangement for the safekeeping of the photo album, finding new accommodation for our dog Pityu and finally preparing for departure by train the following morning, to travel west to the part of Slovakia where Jews were still allowed to live. My uncle Karči and aunt Manci, moved to a small village in that part of Slovakia some months ago where they became the sole dispensers of dental care for miles around. I no longer remember the name of that small village but I know that the closest sizable town was Topoľčany.

We arrived in the small village after dark. We were expected and were welcomed warmly by Manci and Karči. My aunt Manci hugged and kissed me for what seemed a very long time. They had rented a house where one of the rooms contained the dental chair and a pedal-operated drill that they shipped from Hummene. An adjacent room served as the waiting area. We all knew that we were far from safe there. We were required to register with the authorities as newly relocated Jews.

My uncle and his wife Manci were highly skilled dentists and their reputation spread rapidly throughout the region. They treated the dental problems of the people in the region for very small fees and for those who did not have any money they accepted barter. All day a steady stream of patients came for help, often in exchange for food: baked bread, fruit, eggs and at times even a roasted chicken. The food was very much appreciated, because by early 1944 most food items were rationed and Jews were not issued any ration cards. Most of the food we had to buy on the black market which was risky and expensive.

Counting on the good will of the village mayor, my uncle went to see him and asked him to ignore our presence because we would be staying here only for a short time with him and Manci. The mayor of course understood what was at stake. We did not want to be registered because that would make us eligible for immediate deportation. He told my uncle that as far as he was concerned, we were not in the village. He further assured my uncle that the two policemen who were under his jurisdiction would be told likewise to ignore our presence.

Austere and confined as our lives were, we lived in relative safety for several months, although the threat of deportation was ever present. The broadcasts of the Slovak state radio reported at frequent intervals the number of Jews being deported and heralded almost every day that Slovakia would soon be Jew-free. We also frequently listened to forbidden BBC broadcasts that reported the steady progress of the Russian front toward the border of Slovakia.

I know that we spent most of our time indoors, so as not to attract much attention to our presence. I read a lot, but I don't remember what I read or where I obtained the books.

The period spent in that small village is mostly a blank in my memory.

The Slovak National Uprising

Then, on August 29, 1944, a major event occurred. An announcement came on Slovak state radio that an antifascist uprising was in progress centered in Banská Bystrica, a city approximately in the center of Slovakia and only about 70 miles from Topoľčany. At that point the Russian army was only approximately 30 miles from the northern Slovak border with Poland, but still about 180 miles from where we lived. The uprising was a year in planning by a coalition consisting mainly of communist partisans, social democrats who opposed the fascist government of Slovakia and insurgent factions of the Slovak army. The event was triggered by the entry of the German army into Slovakia. Initially, the armed forces of the uprising consisted of about 20,000 soldiers, made up of defectors from the fascist Slovak army and partisans, many of them Jews who had been fighting in the mountains and had now joined the army of the uprising. Mobilization was declared and the army of the uprising shortly grew to about 60,000.

It was immediately clear that we had to reach Banská Bystrica. That night we packed our small suitcases and a knapsack each. All else, including the dental equipment, had to be left behind. Early the following morning, we hired a horse-drawn wagon to take us to the Topoľčany railroad station which was crowded with soldiers and civilians heading for Banská Bystrica. Surprisingly, there were more or less regular train services. In retrospect, I find it surprising that throughout the turmoil of war and bombings, trains by and large continued to run. It was not possible to count on an exact schedule, but if you got to a railroad station, eventually a train would arrive that would be heading in the direction you wanted to go. The train heading for Banská Bystrica arrived early afternoon. I remember the time because I was hungry and my mother gave me a sandwich she packed for the trip.

After a two-hour train ride, we arrived in the Banská Bystrica railroad station. Banská Bystrica is a beautiful town of medieval origin with several well-preserved medieval buildings. At the time of the uprising the population of the town was about 20,000.

Crowds of people who had been hiding from the fascist government were arriving at the station from all parts of Slovakia and from Hungary and Poland. Finding a place to stay turned out to be relatively easy. Many locals were at the station offering to rent rooms in their apartments and houses. We rented a room near the center of town. Manci and Karči rented a room in a farmer's house at the outskirts of the city. This turned out to be a life-saving choice for them.

As soon as we settled in our new dwelling, my father left for the army recruiting office. He was issued a uniform, part of the supplies that over the past year had been stashed for the uprising. He was an experienced truck driver, having learned the skills running his lumber yard. The army assigned him to drive a large truck providing supplies to the front lines.

The following morning, Ignac came by with his truck. I have never seen a truck like that. At its back was a boiler with a pile of wood next to it. A soldier made sure the fire under the boiler was kept burning. I later learned that toward the end of the war, due to a severe shortage of gasoline, most of the gasoline-burning trucks used by the Axis were converted to wood burners.[1]

At first, the uprising was highly successful and within a few days the Slovak national uprising controlled about half of Slovakia. These were exciting, thrilling and hopeful times. The city square was filled with people talking, and listening to the loudspeakers that were broadcasting the initially good news coming from the battlefield. The International Song became the unofficial anthem of the uprising and was sung on frequent occasions. The song is uploaded on You Tube under "International Song in Slovak". Whenever I hear this song I am taken back to the initial heady feelings of the uprising.

Soon the situation changed drastically. The Slovak National Uprising was one of two large centrally organized armed oppositions to the Germans and the local fascist regimes in the German-occupied lands. The other was the uprising in the city of Warsaw. Both were initiated around the same time, at the end of summer 1944, with the aim of the armies of the uprising joining forces with the rapidly approaching Soviet Red Army. These uprisings were encouraged by the Soviet Government, but both were then betrayed by Stalin who did not want the uprisings to succeed. He did not want an independent government in Poland or Slovakia competing with the subservient governments he planned to install. As soon as the uprisings started, the Soviet armies stopped advancing and blocked the bulk of the supplies from reaching the armies of the uprising.

The Germans brought in substantial reinforcements. Forty thousand Waffen SS were brought to Slovakia to reinforce the fascist Slovak army and the German soldiers already present. They mustered a massive offensive and began to squeeze the Army of the Uprising towards Banská Bystrica, systematically annihilating any opposition encountered on the way.

At this point it was clear that the Jews would be the main target for deportation and murder by the invading fascist forces. We had to get out of Banská Bystrica. Ignac still had to complete delivery of supplies to the remaining defenders. He told my mother to take the train to a small town called Jelenec that was planned to be the last holdout of the uprising. There we would meet him and my aunt and uncle and decide what to do. The remaining forces of the uprising were planning to gather in this town to protect the region, provide an opportunity for people to escape into the forest, join partisan groups, or in some way or another escape being arrested by the Germans or fascist Slovak agents.

A problem arose by me developing a severe cough. A physician who, with his family, rented a room next door to us, suggested I had most likely the whooping cough. This of course caused a lot of concern because we might have to hide and my loud coughing would give us away. The physician reassured us that since we would be moving to a completely new environment the whooping cough would likely subside. I don't think that this is a medical fact, but as it turned out my coughing did stop once we left Banská Bystrica. In retrospect, I would guess that the physician's diagnosis of whooping cough was not correct.

My mother once again packed our suitcases and we walked to the railroad station near the center of town. The train that was heading to our destination was packed full of people and was ready to depart, but the doors were still open. My mother and I walked up the car steps determined to board.

A thin tall young man with a sharp gaunt face blocked our way and began to shove us off the steps, screaming anti-Jewish invectives. We barely managed to hold on with both hands to the banister of the train. Finally, some people pulled him away from the door and we squeezed into the train. I can still get in touch with the evil and hatred emanating from that man. He is almost certainly dead by now, but I can summon up his image and the rage, fear and powerlessness he imposed on me.

After a couple of hours of a slow ride, the train came to a stop at a small station. This was the end of the line. The station was full of people trying to decide on the next move. We had no difficulty locating my father, my aunt and uncle. I don't know how they got there, but my guess is that my father picked up Manci and Karči in his truck and drove them there.

We had only two ways to head out of the train station. A paved road that led in the direction from which we came. The other road, unpaved and narrow, led out of the village into the lower Tatra forests and mountains. Everybody realized that to escape the approaching fascist soldiers this was the road to take. We began to walk; a long line of refugees, up that road toward the forest. We were a mixed group made of Jews, soldiers who fought in the uprising and civilians who had heard of the murderous acts of German soldiers in Poland and the Ukraine and realized that the invading German soldiers were desperate and life-threatening.

This long line of refugees, consisting of people on foot, wagons pulled mostly by lone horses and a few ancient automobiles, was making its slow way up the road heading toward the mountains. We were walking for about two hours, the road getting narrower and steeper, when we heard the sound of an approaching airplane. It was a low-flying German plane, examining the scene. Everybody looked at the plane and followed its trajectory. The plane executed a large circle, came back and started to fire its machine gun at us. Chaos ensued immediately. People ran off the road. Horses pulling wagons panicked, overturning the wagons. My mother dragged me off the road and we ran into a gully on the side of the road. Instinctively we threw ourselves on the ground and flattened our bodies behind bushes as best as we could. Bullets were hitting the ground all around me. I wore a red scarf around my neck, its ends spread around me. Suddenly one of the bullets shot from the plane went through my scarf. My mother, thinking that the scarf was used by the pilot as a target pulled the scarf off my neck and threw it into the bushes. The plane made two more passes strafing the road and then flew away. I don't know if anybody was killed. The road at this point was filled with the animals, overturned wagons and abandoned baggage. We got back on the road and continued walking up the road as fast as we could.

I later learned that strafing roads with evacuating civilians was a technique developed by the Germans during the Spanish Civil War. Shooting up these roads produced roadblocks that slowed the transportation of supplies or reinforcements to the troops opposing the Germans. I found the photograph below with the caption shown on the website describing the Slovak National Uprising. It is the scene as I remember it.

We trudged up the road most of the day. The road narrowed and became more or less just a path. The line of refugees had thinned, and in the late afternoon we came to the end of the path which dead ended at the edge of a thick forest.

Here were scattered some very poor, ramshackle houses inhabited by peasants who eked out a living from raising some crops and chickens. In the meadow past the houses about 100 people milled around, soldiers, partisans and refugee families.

It seems that my father had previously made arrangements with one of the farmers for us to use their kitchen and to stay overnight in their house. The farmer and his wife were very welcoming. They were part of the large Hungarian minority living in Slovakia and as was the case with my parents, in private, they spoke Hungarian with each other.

Chaos during the retreat of soldiers and civilians into the mountains north of Banská Bystrica after a machine gun attack by German planes (Source unknown)

One memory from that time and place remains with me vividly. I was at the edge of the meadow watching the scene. A group of partisans together with a few Slovak soldiers were guarding about 50 German soldiers that they had captured at one time or another. The German soldiers had their hands clasped on top of their heads. I heard the partisans debating in Slovak what to do with these prisoners. They were heading into the mountains and they could not take them along. After some loud discussions, they marched the prisoners into the forest. After a while I heard machinegun fire and then the partisans and Slovak soldiers returned without the Germans. I knew that they had been shot, and I went back into the house.

We were all very hungry. My mother bought a few eggs and butter from the farmer to make us an omelet. She commented that it would be nice to have some mushrooms with which to extend the omelet. My father and I went out of the house into a cold and drizzly late afternoon to gather some mushrooms. We walked up a narrow path into the woods. There were plenty of mushrooms all around us and we very quickly filled a small basket with them. We walked back into the kitchen where my mother cleaned the mushrooms, cut them up into small pieces and mixed them with the eggs to cook the omelet. However, as the omelet was cooking she had second thoughts. She asked my father, "Are you sure none of the mushrooms are poisonous?" My father looked taken aback. Clearly, he was not certain. After a pause he answered that he did not take into consideration that some of the mushrooms could have been poisonous. My mother said that the only safe thing to do was to throw out the omelet.

In Hungarian, poisonous mushrooms are called *bolond gomba* literally "crazy mushrooms" or crazy-making mushrooms. The farmer's wife was in the kitchen when my mother suggested that we should throw out the omelet, but she asked my mother not to do that. A nephew of hers lived just a few houses away, and everybody knew that he was already crazy. Therefore, eating crazy mushrooms would not hurt him. My mother agreed to save the omelet for the nephew. The woman left to get the boy and returned with him a few minutes later. He was a large young man looking disheveled and talking some sort of gibberish to himself. He looked a bit scary. Without greeting anyone he sat down on the bench, picked up a fork, and devoured the whole omelet. He got up from the table and without a word walked out into the cold night. The woman gave us some extra bread and butter and that was our supper.

Into the Forest

We got up the following morning at dawn and headed into the forest. We had only our knapsacks now since the suitcases were left behind. It was drizzling and cold on this dreary day in late October. We were a small group consisting of my father, mother, Karči and Manci. As far as I could tell, our plan was to meet some group of partisans who would help us hide in the woods and make our way toward the Russian front where we would be liberated.

Before entering the dark wet forest, my father went up to a group of soldiers to ask about the possibility of joining them in the forest. After talking to several of the soldiers, he came back and told us that these soldiers were not heading for the woods. They planned to disperse, throw away their weapons and uniforms, change into civilian clothing, and merge with other civilians who were on the roads trying to escape the fighting. They were hoping not to get arrested. Any person who had been in the army of the uprising, if caught by the Germans or the Slovak fascists, faced immediate execution.

There was no other choice, we had to head into the forest by ourselves. A young Jewish couple, husband and wife, came over to our little family group and asked if they could join us. My father Ignac, who clearly became our leader, explained to them that we did not have any specific plans but if they wanted to come along they could do so.

We started to walk up a path into the forest, that my father said had been used by loggers for many years. It became evident very soon that we were not prepared for such a trip on a cold rainy day in late October. We all had some type of a raincoat, but our clothing was unsuited for the weather. My shoes got soaked through almost as soon as we started walking on the muddy path. We had very little food with us, and somehow we forgot to bring any water to drink. I was not hungry, but very soon became very thirsty. Fortunately, the barks of the trees served as conduit for the rainwater. So, with patience, and with our tongues on the bark of the tree, we could channel enough water into our mouths to satiate our thirst.

We, that is our small group, walked for a long time up the path without meeting anyone. Walking was especially difficult for my aunt and uncle who were not in good physical shape. After several hours of walking, suddenly three men appeared on the path in front of us. I remember them as the most impressive men I had ever seen. All three wore leather jackets, leather caps and sturdy leather boots. I was aware of their boots because of my flimsy footwear. They had submachine guns slung over their shoulders and knapsacks on their backs. My father had a long conversation with them. One of the men pulled out a handgun from a holster on his belt, raised it over his head and fired one shot into the air. This appeared to have been a signal, because shortly after four more men came out of the woods. This group we met consisted of Jewish partisans looking for recruits. After some discussion the men decided that they wanted my father and mother to join them, but not my aunt and uncle, nor the young couple, and certainly not me. Of course, my parents did not agree to this and the partisans went back into the woods and we continued up the path. We met two other small groups of partisans, but as before, they were willing to take my mother and father, but no one else from our group.

Clearly, our plan was not going to work. We could not survive in the forest, and we could not join a partisan group. We had to get back to Banská Bystrica and hope to survive with our false Arian documents. We continued to walk up the path that, after a short while, forked into two. We took the left branch that my father said would take us to a main road. By now it was getting dark and colder. We were still deep in the forest. The rain had stopped, and this had eased the discomfort of our situation, but it also eliminated our source of drinking water. We had to get out of the woods, but we had to wait until the morning to do that. Ignac retrieved some dry wood from under protruding tree roots and from the sheltered portions of large boulders. He managed to light a smoky fire in a small clearing in the woods, and arranged some wet logs around the fire to sit on. That fire provided us with some warmth for most of the night.

I dozed on and off, but I do remember one episode that occurred during that night. The young man of the couple that joined us was very despondent. In his hands he held two grenades that he picked up along the way. The woods were full of abandoned weapons of various types. He kept saying over and over that our situation was hopeless, that we would be caught by the Germans, so we should just end it right there and throw the grenades into the fire and kill ourselves. After he continued in this vein for some time, my father got up from his log, went to the man and asked him to come with him away from the fire. Later, he must have told us about their conversation because I knew what had transpired. Ignac told him that we were not yet ready to give up, but if he and his wife wanted to kill themselves, my father would build them a separate fire at some distance away from us and he could toss the grenades into his own fire. The man quieted down and returned to our group.

The following morning as soon as there was sufficient light, my father told us to get moving. We had to get to the main road as soon as possible in order to arrive in Banská Bystrica before dark. There was a problem; overnight my aunt Manci lost her sight. Whether it was from the smoke, or from some type of hysterical blindness response, we did not know, but she really couldn't see. I am still surprised as I think back on the events, but nobody seemed panicked. My uncle Karči, her husband, reassured her that her eyesight would return. We quickly gathered our few belongings and started to walk. We took turns holding Manci's hand and guiding her. When I took my turn to guide Manci, we came to a small gully. I carefully lead her down the gully and then helped her climb up. I felt very useful and effective in this role. As the day progressed, Manci's sight gradually returned and by early afternoon she could again walk on her own.

At one point during our trekking through the woods, I was walking ahead of our small group. We came to a meadow, a large cleared space with a remnant of stubs, probably a result of old lumbering activity. Everywhere I looked, I saw weapons, submachine guns, rifles, bayonets, and discarded uniforms. Likely a platoon of soldiers had used this place to decommission themselves from the army of the uprising. I picked up a submachine gun. I can still feel its heft, and although I had only a vague idea how to use this weapon, holding it gave me a great sense of freedom and power. This lasted only a few seconds. Almost immediately my mother ran to me, grabbed the weapon and threw it into the bushes. She told me not to pick up another weapon. She said that if a German patrol were to come by and see me with a weapon, they would shoot our whole group.

Ignac walked ahead, trying to find the right path. Finally, he found a path out of the woods that led us to a road. We joined a small group of people that seemed to know where they were going. I remember being wet and very tired. Puddles of rainwater had gathered in the potholes scattered over the road. When I looked down I saw a torn soaked bag in one of the puddles. The printing on the bag was still legible: 1 kilogram sugar. The sugar had spilled out, was dissolving in the water and had started to mix with the mud.

Soon we came to a small town where amazingly a train was waiting at the station to take off for Banská Bystrica. We got to Banská Bystrica before nightfall. At this point we all had to assume our false Arian identities immediately. We found out that the order to deport all Jews to concentration camps from German-controlled lands was being actively implemented with great zeal. We all had to separate. Once again, renting rooms was easy. Paying jobs were scarce, so most people were eager to obtain additional income from renting part of their home.

My mother and I rented a room in the old section of Banská Bystrica in a boarding house owned by a middle-aged man who had only one leg. The other one had been amputated because of an injury he sustained in WWI. He was a widower and lived alone in an old house without indoor plumbing. A hand-pump operated a well and an outhouse was situated in his neglected garden, overgrown with tall weeds. At this point we were his only customers. Our small rented room had one narrow bed where my mother and I slept together. I was frightened of our new landlord who usually scowled and had an angry expression on his face.

Occasionally, he smiled when he saw my mother, but he seemed to dislike me. He had a prosthetic leg that he rarely wore. Usually it was hanging from a hook on the hall. Most of the time he used crutches to walk. My father rented a room in a small boarding house several blocks from our rented room, and my aunt and uncle returned to the farmhouse where they had lived during the uprising.

The following day, I went outside into a large fenced backyard adjacent to the boarding house. It was cold and the ground was frozen hard. Four boys – all older than me – were standing in a circle with their penises out of their pants, masturbating. When they saw me they urged me to do as they were doing. I knew what they were doing. They wanted to see if my penis was circumcised which would reveal that I was a Jew and they might collect some reward. When their urgings grew more insistent, I ran back into the house and told my mother what had happened. My mother examined my penis, pulled the skin down over the tip and managed to cover the tip of the penis and squeezed the skin together, hoping that it would stay together. This maneuver did not work. As soon as she let go, the skin popped up again. There was no way around this. My mother cautioned me to keep my penis always hidden, but I already knew that.

Decades later, when I was enrolled in high school in Canada, I was astounded to see in the shower following the gym class, that nearly all boys – Jews, and non-Jews – were circumcised. A deadly giveaway in Europe was of no consequence here.

My mother joined the library and brought home books both for herself and for me. I spent most of the day reading. She and Ignac had arranged for us to meet for about 20 minutes or so every afternoon in one of the small parks or open public spaces scattered throughout the town. Sometimes we walked to those meeting, but often we took a bus. Meetings with my father were the highlight of my day.

The death of Ignac

We settled into this routine that continued for about a month. One day in early December (later I found out it was December 7, 1944), my mother and I were sitting on a bench in a park, waiting for Ignac. We waited for more than an hour, but he did not come. My mother was distraught and I was also very upset and scared. We both knew that he must have been caught and arrested. The entire following day, we sat on a bench in a small park across from the building that doubled as the police station and the city jail, hoping to get some information about the fate of Ignac. In retrospect, this may not have been such a wise thing to have done. Had we been noticed and reported, we too would have been arrested.

In the late morning, the large gates of the building opened and a group of about 50 men, surrounded by armed soldiers was marched out. Among them, near the front, was Ignac. My mother jumped up and started to run after them. A chant arose from the group probably initiated by my father, "*Gei avek! Gei avek!* Go away! Go away!" My mother stopped running after the group and returned to the park bench where I was sitting. She held me in her arms and sobbed for a long time.

After the war, my mother and I returned briefly to Banská Bystrica and the two of us went to the police station to inquire about Ignac. The clerk at the front desk was painfully rude. In responding to my mother's question he answered that Ignac was certainly dead and that too many of us Jews survived anyway.

In July 2018, I got a voicemail from Dušan Hudec, a filmmaker and producer in Bratislava. He asked whether I could return his call because he had some news about Ignac. Of course, I called him back immediately. Hudec was gathering information about the killing of 900 people, mostly Jews, captured in and around Banská Bystrica after the Slovak National Uprising.

The fascist Slovak authorities kept detailed entries of the people they captured. Among the records, he found the name of my father Ignac Mandel. A separate entry shows the date of his imprisonment as December 7, 1944.

Police arrest record of my father Ignac Mandel.

Some years earlier, while I was in Jerusalem visiting Yad Vashem, the Holocaust museum in Israel, I filled out a form listing my relatives murdered during the Holocaust. I listed Ignac Mandel as my stepfather. This entry led him to phone and tell me the details of how Ignac had been killed.

By the end of December 1944, the Banská Bystrica prison held about 900 prisoners captured after the uprising – men, women and children, nearly all Jews. The captors began to kill the prisoners on January 4, 1945. During the following week, they killed most of the prisoners in captivity. While they kept clean and detailed records of the capture of the prisoners, the authorities that were in charge of the murders tried to keep the killings secret. They transported the captives by bus to the outskirts of a nearby village called Nemecká, about 14 miles from Banská Bystrica.

The outskirts of Nemecka housed a lime kiln.[2] It was here that the victims were shot and then thrown into the burning kiln. The executioners threw pitch into the burning fire to mask the smell of burning flesh. It has been reported that often babies were thrown into the fire alive to conserve bullets. Initially the murders were conducted by a joint force of German *Einsatzkommando* and members of Slovak regime's Hlinka Guard, but later the murders were taken over entirely by the Slovak Hlinka Guard. The soldiers were told to keep the murders strictly secret, but the killing quickly became common knowledge. After the murders of the day the soldiers drank in the local bars and boasted about their deeds. Most days the soldiers went from door to door in the surrounding villages, selling the items they had stolen from the murdered victims.

After my father was marched away to what we now know was his death, my mother and I tried to resume our lives in Banská Bystrica. But two events in quick succession forced us to be on the run again. The person who rented to us the single room was a nasty angry man who somehow blamed the loss of his leg on the Jews. He hated Jews with a venomous passion. However, he did lust after my mother. A few days after the arrest of my father, he told my mother that he believed she was a Gentile woman, but he was sure that I was not her nephew and that I was a Jewish boy she was sheltering. He said he had been watching me and whenever I went to the outhouse I always took a book with me, and nobody but a Jewish kid would go to an outhouse and read. My mother feigned outrage and told him that she would go to the police and accuse him of harassment. I vaguely remember that there was a law against falsely accusing someone of being a Jew and this threat seems to have quieted him down for a couple of days.

But there was another problem looming. The landlord had registered my mother as a tenant in his house. As a result, she had to present herself the following morning at the police station to have her identity card validated. This was not an unusual event, still it caused us a lot of anxiety. Early in the morning we went to the police station to have our documents validated. We were among the first people present, and soon my mother's name was called. Both my mother and I were escorted into a small office where a large uniformed policeman sat behind a desk. We sat on wooden chairs and I remember my feet did not reach the floor and were awkwardly dangling in the air. My mother passed her identity papers to the policeman who leaned back in his chair and looked at them for a long time. Then he looked at my mother and said, "I know you are not Anna Hricakova. Anna and I come from the same village and I was her lover for almost a year. But you are a beautiful woman and I want to help you. If you come and live with me, I will protect you and your boy."

My mother feigned enthusiasm and gratefulness and said she would pack up our belongings and meet him in front of the building in the afternoon. Meanwhile could he validate her identity card. He did that. On the way out I asked my mother what this all meant. She explained very simply that the policeman wanted my mother to act as his wife. In very simple terms she explained what this meant and I more or less understood it. She said that she would never do that and that this was very dangerous for us.

We rushed back to our rented room, quickly packed up our few belongings and took the streetcar to the railway station. My mother bought tickets for the first train out of Banská Bystrica which was headed for Bratislava, the capital city of Slovakia.

9

BRATISLAVA

The train arrived in Bratislava in the late evening. All passengers, and we together with them got off the train and walked down a set of stairs into the large, high-domed waiting room. I remember the distinct feeling of fear and displacement. Everybody seemed to be walking purposefully with a clear destination. Some had friends waiting for them welcomingly. We had no place to go. We were in Bratislava only because this was the final destination of the train. I remember the cavernous hall and a large clock on the far wall showing a few minutes past 11 o'clock. Neither of us had ever been in Bratislava and we had no idea where to go nor what was beyond those doors people passed through.

Bratislava was the capital of Slovakia. When we arrived at the end of 1944 it had a population of about 200,000. Neither my mother nor I had ever been in such a large city. We did not want to attract attention by being conspicuously confused, still we had no choice. The two of us sat down on one of the many polished benches with our two little suitcases by our feet. The row of passengers leaving the station through the large doors thinned, and soon we were nearly alone. A young woman, I later found out she was 22 years old, carrying a suitcase, looked at us and came over. "You look like you need some help. Do you have a place to stay?" she asked. "We don't," my mother answered. "You can stay with me," she responded. As I remember it, she told us her name was Helena.

We picked up our suitcases and followed her out the door into the snowy cold. We took the streetcar, got off somewhere in the center of town, and walked to her apartment house. The snow banks were nearly as tall as I was, with interconnecting trenches which Helena said were made by children as part of some hide and seek game. I remember most clearly the street sign *Židovska Ulica*, Jewish street. This was part of what had been the old medieval Jewish Ghetto.

The history of Jews in Bratislava mirrors that of many European communities. Jews had come to the area in the 11th century as tradesmen and traders. Jewish presence was made official in 1291 in the municipal charter that gave Jews the right to reside within city walls. Local upheavals always brought troubles for the Jews. From my childhood I remember the Slovak saying *Ked bida tak do Žida* ("When there is trouble attack the Jews"). In 1596, after a lost battle with the Ottomans, the Jews were expelled from Slovak cities including Bratislava. A hundred years later, as regional events quieted down, Jews began to return and rebuild their communities. When in December 1944, we walked on Židovska Ulica there were no more Jews living openly in Slovakia. I remember how strange it felt to see that sign *Židovska Ulica*. Here we were, first continually abused verbally because we were Jews, now our lives were in danger because we were Jews whom they wanted to obliterate, and here was a street openly identified in our name.

Decades later, when I visited Bratislava with my son Michael, we found only a few traces of this neighborhood. Most of it had been demolished to make way for a new bridge crossing the Danube. Bratislava had now grown to a city of about 400,000 people, but small as the city was, it gave the impression of being much larger. The city had a long association with Hungarian and Austrian nobility who, over the decades, built many impressive mansions, theaters, concert halls, monuments, and spacious parks.

Helena lived in one small room of a two-room apartment that she shared with an older woman. The two rooms were in series. From the hall we walked directly into Helena's room that was connected to the second one, occupied by her roommate. The kitchen was adjacent to the second room with the bathroom accessible from the kitchen. When we came in, late as it was, Helena's roommate was sitting at an upright piano playing a beautiful piece, *Für Elise*. She barely acknowledged our entrance and I don't remember her ever speaking to us or to Helena. Helena told us that the woman was a piano teacher, but that very few could now afford piano lessons. It is my impression that she sat at the piano all day playing *Für Elise* over and over again.

That melody still evokes the feeling of that time, the entry from the bitter cold to a warm shelter, and the relief given by a semblance of safety this room provided. Helena's room contained a double bed that filled most of the space and a small round table with three chairs around it.

That night, and for the following two months, the three of us slept together in that bed, with Helena on one side, my mother on the other, and I in the middle. I still remember how her night gown hiked up and I felt her naked behind against my body. Every night *Für Elise* came from next door as the piano teacher played on into the night.

By the time we arrived in Bratislava, we were nearly out of money. The only possession we had that could be sold was a Leica camera that had belonged to my uncle Karči and somehow found itself in our possession. Helena told us of a place at the edge of a park near the city center where such items could be sold or traded. So the day after our arrival my mother and I took the streetcar to that park and, after speaking to a few strangers who were standing around and seemed to be acting as middlemen for transactions, a tall young man approached us and bought the camera. On our way home we stopped at a butcher's and bought meat for dinner. We had no ration cards, so we paid the black-market price that, I remember my mother saying, was much higher than in Banska Bystrica.

We ate most of our meals together with Helena, while my mother and Helena took turns cooking. Occasionally Helena's male friend joined us, bringing some additional supplies. My mother and Helena became good friends, spending a lot of time together. From their quiet conversation I deduced that Helena had frequent problems with her boyfriend and my mother served as an advisor and confidante.

A few days after we arrived in Bratislava, we saw a 'help wanted' sign in a small tailor shop nearby. The two of us walked in and found a middle-aged, somewhat pudgy man operating a sewing machine. The man got up and greeted us. In answer to my mother's question he told us that he was the owner of the shop and needed an assistant. My mother told him that she would like the job. He asked my mother to demonstrate her skills with some sewing on of buttons, and hemming a skirt. After about half an hour he gave her the job. My mother then stipulated that I had to stay with her while she worked and that I would be very quiet. That was not hard for me. Helena worked in a bookstore and she brought home several books for me to read. When I finished one group, she brought another so that I always had a supply of reading material. I spent most of my time reading. And that is what I did, sitting in the corner of the tailor shop.

One Sunday afternoon, as a special treat, my mother bought tickets to a movie that was advertised to be some fairy tale such as "Snow White". But when we sat down, and the hall darkened, for some reason, a different film was substituted. A German propaganda film showing rehabilitation of wounded German soldiers with prosthetic arms frolicking in a swimming pool. I remember one particular procedure featured with pride in the documentary. Due to an explosion a soldier's hands had to be amputated. The two bones joining the hand to the elbow, the radius and the ulna, were separated by cutting them apart. The muscles and tendons were rearranged so that the two bones formed a pincer-like arrangement. The wounded soldier could now pick up and manipulate objects held between the two bones that could move with respect to each other. He could even hold a cigarette with his reconstructed arm. The procedure and its results made me queasy. I kept hoping that this was only a brief news reel and that the promised feature would begin. It never did. When the documentary ended, we walked out into the cold early winter darkness.[1]

In our second month in Bratislava, an elderly German soldier walked into the tailor shop bringing several pairs of trousers to alter and clean. He noticed my mother and came over to say hello. They spoke for a few minutes. He asked some questions in fragmented Slovak while my mother pretended to speak only rudimentary German. She told me that he was an orderly for a high-level Gestapo officer. Next day he came back and brought us a loaf of bread and some butter. For the remainder of our stay in Bratislava, this elderly soldier came to the shop several times, always bringing some food for us: usually bread, and sometimes cheese or salami.

Our relatively peaceful stay in Bratislava came to an abrupt end in mid-February, 1945. As usual, my mother was altering some garment and I sat quietly in the corner reading one of the books Helena brought from the store when a sharply dressed German officer, in the company of the orderly whom we had gotten to know, walked in. He spoke with my mother for a while after which he and the orderly departed. The officer had invited us for a dinner that he was hosting that evening. We would be picked up by the orderly in the early evening. We dressed up as well as we could. My mother ironed my pants and her skirt which is about the most we could do with what we had.

The orderly picked us up promptly at 6 in the evening in the fanciest car I have ever seen. After a short ride we arrived at a large house with a circular driveway. The orderly opened the car door for us and two servants ushered us into the mansion. We were the first to arrive and the Gestapo officer took my mother and me on a tour of "his" house, wanting to show it off. I can still visualize details such as the wide staircases, beautiful rugs and works of art. Later I found out from my mother that the mansion had belonged to a prosperous Jewish merchant, who – together with his family – was deported to Auschwitz.

Two more German officers with their girlfriends arrived and we sat down to dinner. We were served by two waiters. I don't recall what we had for dinner, but I distinctly remember thinking that I had perhaps never eaten so well and plentifully before.

After dinner, the officer asked my mother to join him in the living room. She came out a few minutes later and dessert was served. We were then driven home. My mother told me that the German officer made her a similar offer to the one the policeman in Banská Bystrica had made. My mother accepted and told him she would be back the following evening. She told me we would leave Bratislava early in the morning the next day. When we got back to Helena's apartment, she was still up eager to know what happened. By now Helena knew that we were Jews, so our decision to leave as soon as possible came as no surprise to her. The next morning Helena took the streetcar with us to the train station and my mother bought tickets for us on an early morning train out of Bratislava. This happened to be a train to Žilina, a city about 120 miles north east of Bratislava. My mother and I consulted on the destination and I suggested that the closer we would move east and north toward the Polish border the more likely we would be liberated by the approaching Soviet army. A train heading toward Žilina was leaving shortly. It seemed like a perfect destination, a relatively large city in the right geographic direction.

While trains were kept running during the war, the schedules were unreliable. Frequently railroad tracks were destroyed by bombing or sabotage, and often fuel shortages stopped the trains. This time our train to Žilina was rerouted to a small town called Turčianske Teplice.

The conductor announced that the train was delayed for an unknown period of time because of track problems. Including my mother and me about ten people got off the train, and we headed for the small restaurant adjacent to the waiting room. When we entered, the restaurant was empty except for two uniformed policemen eating their breakfast at a table by the window facing the railroad tracks. The restaurant had only a few tables and they were close together. We sat down at a table one removed from the policemen, and my mother ordered us something to eat. There was not much of a choice. I think we had some bread, cheese and tea.

In times of peace, Turčianske Teplice was a popular spa town with waters that had the reputation of healing a variety of conditions.[2] However, at this time of turmoil, the town had a population of only about 1,500 people. This was too small a town for us to remain unnoticed and unsuspected. We had to move on as soon as possible. My mother got up, told me I should wait while she went to the ticket office to find out if there was a way to continue our trip to Žilina.

One of the policemen got up and came to me. "*Du redst Yiddish?*" I understood the question: "Do you speak Yiddish?" Obviously, the purpose of the question was to find out if we were Jews. I answered, "I don't understand what you said."

The policeman returned to his table, sat down and said to his partner in a quiet voice, but one I could hear. "I know this woman and the boy are Jews, but I really want to help them." The second policeman said something to the effect that this was alright with him.

At this point, it was evident to most people in Slovakia that the German and the Slovak fascist governments were on the verge of defeat. The fate of Jews that had lived among them was also known to nearly everybody, although a large fraction of the population was still set on killing all Jews they could find. Whether out of guilt, compassion or fear, people were less prone to participate in the murders, and more likely to help Jews to survive.

Shortly after, my mother returned to the restaurant and sat down next to me. She looked disturbed, and told me that no one had any idea when we could get out of Turčianske Teplice. The schedule depended on how quickly the track could be repaired and because we were not on a main line, the track repair was not a priority.

I told her that I needed to go to the toilet and asked whether she would come with me. The toilets were in another building outside the restaurant. As soon as we were outside, I told my mother about the conversation between the two policemen and I told her that we could probably trust them.

We returned to the restaurant and sat back down at our table. The policeman who had previously come to talk to me, now came over to speak with my mother. He told her, as she already knew, that we were stuck in Turčianske Teplice – nobody knew for how long. But he could take us to a small village called Rakša that was under his jurisdiction, where we would be safe most likely till the end of the war. My mother accepted his offer and thanked him. He said that he had to leave the police car with his colleague. In any case, the path that led to Rakša was not suitable for a car, but we could walk to Rakša in less than two hours. The policeman placed the rifle across his shoulder, picked up our two small suitcases and we started on the narrow path, more like a hiking trail, to Rakša.

10

RAKŠA

After about an hour and a half of walking, we arrived in Rakša, a tiny primitive village with small houses that had thatched roofs and walls of dried mud bricks. Somehow, I remember that the population of Rakša at that time was about 100 people. Small fenced plots surrounded each house. Chickens ran around, and some houses had a small barn with a cow or horse in it. Rakša had no roads leading to it except for that path we took from Turčianske Teplice. It had no electricity, no plumbing and certainly no telephones – virtually no contact with the outside world. I later learned that farmers from Rakša took whatever excess produce they had – vegetables, chickens, an occasional pig – to the local market in Turčianske Teplice once a week and shopped in the local stores for goods they needed.

When we arrived, there was considerable activity in the village; Men and women feeding animals, people clearing snow from the paths that connected the houses that were built not on laid-out streets, but scattered helter-skelter. The people we met looked at us with curiosity, but all seemed to know the policeman and greeted him as a friend.

The policeman took us straight to a house that was a bit larger than most, and told us that this was the home of the mayor of the village. The mayor came out of his house to greet the policeman and invited us in. The policeman told the mayor that we were his personal friends, almost like family. "I want you to take care of them and I'll hold you personally responsible for their well-being," he said and then left.

The mayor asked my mother if she had money to pay rent. My mother confirmed that we did have some money. The mayor took us to a small house at the far end of the group of houses that comprised Rakša. In the house was one single large room which served as a kitchen and bedroom for the woman who lived there. Soon, we learned that she was the local prostitute. She was pleasant to us, brought in a mattress that was to be our bed and an old quilt. She hung two sheets from the ceiling to separate out a space for us.

Soon it became evident that having a child living with her was a problem since it interfered with her business. I remember a few times when we had to leave the house in the evening and had to walk around till things were finished in her part of the room. This was in the winter, and – in my rather flimsy clothing – I remember being very cold when waiting outside.

My mother and our prostitute host went to speak to the mayor and explained to him that this wasn't working. The mayor promised to find another arrangement. The next day, he took us to another house where we actually got a small room of our own in this family's tiny house. Everybody in Rakša was very poor, but seemed to be generous and in good spirits.

At this point we had run out of money, but here again my mother used her skills as a seamstress. She took in clothing to repair and alter and in return customers brought us food. I remember we shared food and ate together with the family in whose house we lived.

In peacetime the children from Rakša attended school in Turčianske Teplice, sometimes having to walk there or occasionally being taken in someone's horse and wagon. But now school was closed and the children were mostly on their own. I made some friends among the boys in the village. We played together and roamed the hills around Rakša. In this rather peaceful way we lived till mid-April; No stranger ever came to Rakša.

Then one day toward end of April, after we had been in Rakša for about two months, a large Hungarian army convoy came across the field: trucks, tanks, and about 1,000 soldiers. For some reason the joint German-Hungarian command chose the area of Rakša to make a stand against the advancing Russian-Romanian forces. At the start of WWII both Romania and Hungary were allies of Germany, and participated in the invasion of the Soviet Union. In the summer of 1944 as the war progressed and it became evident that Germany was going to be defeated, Romania switched sides and started to fight on the side of the Soviet Union. Hungary, on the other hand, remained an active ally of Germany.

The Hungarian soldiers put up tents and field kitchens, dug trenches, and in preparation for the battle, planted many mines along the access lines in the direction of the expected attack. With the Hungarian soldiers came about a dozen German soldiers mostly very young. The villagers spoke only Slovak. Of course, my mother spoke Hungarian and also reasonably competent German. This was made known and she became the contact between the army and the village, feigning to speak only a few words necessary for communication. She negotiated with the commanding officer – I think he was a colonel – where to set up the army tents, park the vehicles and other details so as to least disturb the life of the village.

The Hungarian colonel was very cooperative, I think mostly because he was almost immediately smitten by my mother. He sought her out frequently during the day to converse with her about some detail or another. My mother always took me with her to diffuse the officer's passion. The conversation between them was very choppy, because my mother pretended to speak only broken Hungarian. At this point there was a severe shortage of food in the village. The army likewise suffered from inadequate food supply, still they had more than we did. The colonel brought us food almost every day, usually bread and canned meat. My mother shared the food with the household where we lived.

One afternoon, my mother and I were sitting on a wooden bench outside the house where we lived, when one of the German soldiers approached us. I guess he heard that my mother understood German. He squatted down to be at our height, and without any prompting words poured out of him. I understood a bit of what he said because I knew some Yiddish, but my mother filled me in later. He was 16 years old, but the German army being desperate for soldiers drafted him when he was still only 15. He was from a small village in Bavaria and he didn't even know what this war was about and now the Russians would come and kill him. He started to cry. He then asked my mother to tell the Russians that he never did anything bad, so they should not kill him. My mother agreed to put in a word for him if she had a chance. He thanked her and left. We never saw him again.

Later that day, the colonel came to speak to my mother, informing her that they would move out of Rakša the following morning to meet the invading forces. He held the money for the monthly pay of all the soldiers in his battalion and wanted to give this money to my mother for safekeeping. The fighting would be over soon and he would come back, marry my mother and the money would be their stake to start a new life. He wanted my mother to promise that she would wait for him. My mother said that she could not marry him, because she was engaged and she did not want to be responsible for all that money. The colonel left disappointed, but said he would be back anyway and my mother should think over her options.

The following morning, we woke up to a loud commotion: tanks, trucks, soldiers all moving out of Rakša. A few hours later, we heard explosions and gun fire. A few shells fell on Rakša and exploded harmlessly in a field outside the village. The bombardment and explosions now came more rapidly. We hid in a root cellar a few feet underground where the family stored its previous season's crop of potatoes, beets, other root vegetables, and wheat.

Explosions and sounds of battle continued through the night and stopped toward morning. We stayed in the cellar until mid-morning when someone outside banged on the door and a Russian soldier came in. He was part of a small contingent in charge of the Romanian troops and we, speaking Slovak, could communicate with him about simple matters. The Hungarian army surrendered and was marched off to a prisoner of war camp. The fighting was over and it was safe for us to come out.

The village was now filled with Romanian soldiers whom, with a few exceptions, nobody could understand. Communication was possible with a few Romanians who came from the geographic region that – from time to time – was under the control of Hungary. They spoke very basic Hungarian. Not surprisingly, the Romanian soldiers were treated very harshly by their Russian overseers and they seemed very eager to connect with the civilian population. Once again, my mother and I formed a point of contact.

I have a few memories from our stay in Rakša, most of them about events that occurred after the war was over. Only a few days after the arrival of the Romanian soldiers, the war in Europe ended. The German Army capitulated on May 7th, 1945. Our liberation in Rakša came late, because the Russian invasion had bypassed most of Slovakia to push forward towards Berlin. We were, of course, eager to leave Rakša and locate our family, but the country was in chaos. Transportation, food distribution, policing were all disrupted. The policeman who brought us to Rakša came to the village as part of the attempt of the local government to stabilize the country region by region. He advised us to wait a few weeks before leaving the village.

A couple of days after the Romanian soldiers came to Rakša, platoons went out to comb the countryside for the bodies of their dead comrades. I don't know what they did with dead Hungarian soldiers; they probably just left them in the field. The fields were filled with dead corpses, dead horses, dead soldiers. A group of boys, I among them, came to the cemetery to watch them bring in the Romanian corpses.

I remember the way they brought in the corpses of the dead soldiers. They had tied their hands and their feet and then put a pole through the two loops at the two ends of the body.

Two soldiers, one on each end, with the poles on their shoulders, brought in the corpses to the cemetery. The poles sagged under the weight of the corpse and bounced in rhythm with each step. The soldiers simply dumped the dead body onto the pile of bodies already collected. One of the soldiers pulled out the pole and the pair went off looking for more corpses. Most of the Romanian soldiers were killed by mines. Their bodies were bloated, their faces bluish grey. The pile of corpses grew. I actually counted them. I forget the exact number, but it was about 30.

As we stood there watching, I noticed that a folding knife was poking out of the trouser pocket of one of the corpses. I had never owned a pocket knife and so I walked close to the pile of bodies and while nobody was looking, I pulled the knife out of the dead soldier's pocket. The knife had two folded blades – one large and one small. I quickly put it into my own pocket. The soldiers had dug a big trench and started to place the corpses into this grave. We boys dispersed.

I went back to where we lived. Night fell. Nights in Rakša of course were very dark, without electricity or any street lights. Before going to bed I had to go to the outhouse and I was very frightened. I felt the weight of the stolen knife in my pocket. I was horrified. What if the ghost of the dead soldier came back to claim his knife?

My mother saw how fearful I was and asked me what happened. I told her about my stealing the knife from the corpse. She reassured me that she knew what to do: "Give me this knife, I'll take care of it for now, and tomorrow we will return it." The following morning my mother and I went to the cemetery. The mass grave was clearly visible. We brought a small trowel and I dug a hole next to the grave. I put the knife in it and covered it. This seemed like the perfect solution.

At this point the Romanian soldiers had very little to do and were just waiting for permission to go home. I befriended one of them who spoke some Hungarian. I don't know why, perhaps because I reminded him of his own son, he gave me a small brass trumpet. He told me that the trumpet was used to summon firemen to put out fires. The trumpet had two valves that when pushed alternately, causing the air blown into the trumpet to produce a siren-like sound.

No matter how poor the village, there is always someone who is richer than anybody else and he is the rich man. In Rakša that was the miller. He lived in a relatively large house next to the creek that flowed through the village and propelled the grinding stones in his mill. He was also the head of the volunteer fire brigade of the village. I went to his house, showed him the trumpet and asked him if he would like to trade it for some flour. He tried out the trumpet and gave me two kilos of flour for it. When I brought this rare commodity home, I got lavish praise from the adults. The family we lived with used some of the flour to bake bread mixing the dough with mashed potatoes. The rest of the flour was traded for other food.

A couple of weeks passed, and things had quieted down. Now it was time for us to leave Rakša. We packed our suitcases and were waiting in front of the house for a farmer with a horse and wagon who was planning to go to Turčianske Teplice and who promised to take us there. We thought we might be able to catch a train to Topoľčany where we hoped to find my uncle and aunt, Karči and Manci – if they survived.

As we were waiting in front of the house, a boy about my age, who was one of my playmates in Rakša, crossed the road, ran up to me and said that he had something very exciting to show me and that I should come with him. I asked my mother if I had the time to do that and she said no, because our ride would be here very shortly. So somewhat disappointed I did not go. He left, and a few minutes later – just as the wagon was approaching – we heard big explosion. The explosion came from the backyard of the boy's house across the road where we were waiting. A few minutes later we saw the boy's father, a tall thin man, coming out of the yard horrified, sobbing, carrying the limp body of his son in his arms. The boy was covered in blood as was his father's shirt. The boy's pants were shredded, his testicles were hanging out, and were attached to his body by only a thin strip of skin. Someone, who seemed to know, said that the boy was dead. He found a grenade, played with it and it exploded. There was nothing anyone could do for him. We climbed on the wagon and left Rakša.

Looking for Rakša

In 1983, my son Michael and I visited Czechoslovakia (now Slovakia). Of course, one of the places I wanted Michael to see was Rakša, where we lived when finally the war ended for us. I was under the firm impression that the town, where the train stopped and from where we walked to Rakša, was called Zlaté Moravce. Rakša, being a tiny village, was not on our map so we drove to Zlaté Moravce where I inquired how we could get to Rakša. We went to the police station, to the post office, and asked several shopkeepers, but we could not find anyone who had heard of Rakša. I began to doubt my memory. Perhaps I mis-remembered the name of the village, but how could that be? We left Zlaté Moravce disappointed.

Several years later, after the fall of the communist regime, I typed into Google "Rakša, Slovakia", and up popped a rather elaborate website extolling the beauty of Rakša and its surroundings. As was stated on the website, Rakša is in fact near Turčianske Teplice, a small town about 25 miles north of Zlaté Moravce. Clearly my memory confused the two towns.

The website made evident the lure of free enterprise, advertising that the small peasant houses I remembered had been converted to vacation dwellings. I recognized some of the houses and locations shown in the posted photographs. The website advertisement for Rakša stated: "Vacation in a place like your grandmother used to live in." The ad went on to say that these small houses have been converted to comfortable "no smoking" vacation places, simple, but close to good restaurants, horseback riding, swimming, tennis and hiking. One could make online reservations for this reasonably priced resort. Unfortunately, the venture seems to have failed as a resort. [1] The population of Rakša is still only about 200.

11

BACK INTO THE WORLD

The farmer who gave us a ride from Rakša let us off at the railroad station in Turčianske Teplice where it became immediately evident that our plan to get a train going toward Topoľčany was not going to work. The station was abandoned, and a man coming from a nearby house told us that for the past month no train has come to, or gone from Turčianske Teplice. At this point we were about 30 miles from Topoľčany and there seemed to be no clear way to get there.

It was now getting dark and cold. We walked towards the center of town which seemed to be teeming with soldiers – both Russian and Romanian – and with civilian refugees like us who were trying to find a way to get back to their homes. It did not feel safe to tell anyone that we were Jews, so we kept our false identity. Two policemen patrolling the streets pointed us to a large house that was abandoned by the owner and his family. They had left Turčianske Teplice for some place they deemed safer in the light of the possible battle that was anticipated. The house itself was filled with soldiers, but in the large yard a bonfire was burning and

Russian soldiers as well as civilians were sitting around the fire. Some of the soldiers were eating their rations, mostly bread, and some type of lard and dried meat. One of the soldiers asked my mother if we were hungry. Of course, we were, and he collected food from some of the soldiers and brought it over to us. A few soldiers brought over straw from the barn and spread it around the fire. Everybody chose a space and laid down as far from each other as we could and still be warmed somewhat by the fire. My mother and I fell asleep.

Shortly after, a Russian soldier snuck over, pinned down my mother and began to molest her. My mother began to scream at him. Several soldiers jumped up and ran over. They pulled the soldier off my mother and warned him to stay away. This he did, but we did not sleep much for the rest of the night.

The following morning, the soldiers gave us some bread and tea in a tin cup. We stood in line to wash our faces at an outdoor pump, and resumed our journey. I don't remember details about our journey to Topoľčany. It consisted of short rides on back of wagons, old trucks, and much walking. I know that we did not get to Topoľčany that same day we started out from Turčianske Teplice. We passed through many small farming villages and several times my mother had to ask for directions to Topoľčany. I don't know where we slept that night when we were still on the road – most likely in a barn of a farmer in one of the many small farming villages we passed through.

On the morning of the following day, we were about seven miles from Topoľčany. We were walking on an unpaved road, actually more like a wide path, rutted, barely suitable for motor traffic. By midday, both my mother and I were very hungry and tired. As we were trudging along this path, we heard a faint engine noise that grew louder and louder. Looking behind us we saw a large cloud of dust out of which emerged a motorcycle. The driver wore a leather helmet and as he zoomed by and passed us, he did not even slow down. Just as he went by us, we saw an object fall out of his rucksack tied on the back of his motorcycle. The object bounced two or three times on the road and then rolled into the roadside ditch. The motorcycle disappeared into the distance. I ran over and picked up the object in the ditch. It was a head of cheese about the size and shape of a honeydew. The cheese was covered by a brown skin and when my mother cut through it, we inhaled the wonderful aroma of the smoked cheese. She cut a small slice for each of us. After about a half an hour of walking we got a ride on the back of an old truck to the next village. Here we found a baker who gave us a loaf of bread for part of our cheese.

After some more walking and a few short rides we arrived in Topoľčany late that afternoon. Amazingly and to our great relief my aunt and uncle, Manci and her husband Karči, were already in the little village near Topoľčany. They were liberated at the end of March 1945, and had arrived about three weeks before we did. They found the little house they had rented from a neighboring farmer with their dental equipment undisturbed and ready for use. Almost immediately they resumed their dental practice and were waiting in the hope that we had survived and would head for the last place where we had lived together.

The joy of our reunion is beyond verbal description. There was much hugging and crying. Most of the talking was done by Manci and my mother telling the saga of our survivals. My aunt prepared a meal of cabbage, potatoes and boiled beef. I can still recall the scent of that meal. In my memory it remains the best meal I ever had.

Every Jew who survived the Holocaust is probably aware of the sequence of remarkable and improbable events that made survival possible. This was certainly so for Manci and Karči. After the defeat of the uprising at the end of October 1944, our little group came down from the forest to a main road leading to Banská Bystrica, we decided to separate, because it would have been dangerously suspicious to stay together. Manci and Karči, having been classified as having a nationally needed skill, assumed they were safe from deportation and did not need to procure false Arian documents as we did. That, of course, was a serious miscalculation.

When we reached Banská Bystrica, Manci and Karči did not know what to do. For lack of any better idea, they went to the house of the family at the edge of the town where they had rented a room during the uprising. They told the family of their predicament and asked for their help. At that point everybody knew that any Jew caught by the Germans or the Slovak fascists would be deported to Auschwitz and killed, and any Gentile harboring Jews would likewise be deported. The family conferred and told Manci and Karči that they were willing to hide them in an old barn in the corner of their back yard. The barn was used as storage space for farm equipment. The barn had an attic accessible by a ladder, where they kept bales of hay. They could make a space in the interior of the attic that would not be visible from the ground level.

My aunt and uncle were of course greatly relieved and thankful. They remained hidden in that space for six months, from the end of October to the end of March when

Banská Bystrica was liberated by the Russian and Rumanian armies. They lay essentially silently on their backs all that time. They could sit up, but the height of the attic did not allow standing up. At night, the members of the family brought them food and took away waste. Had the host family been discovered hiding Jews they would also have been deported and killed. Hiding Manci and Karči became especially dangerous when in January the Germans moved the field kitchen into the backyard only a few meters from the barn. But there were gentiles who took such risks to save a human life. All of us who survived owe our lives to people who were capable of such goodness and bravery.

We heard on the radio that a new Czechoslovak government was formed, but though the fighting had stopped the country was far from functioning. Gasoline was not available, so travel – except for short distances – was not possible. The Slovak currency issued by the fascist government was now worthless, the economy therefore had to be based on barter. The dental practice of my aunt and uncle was very busy so we had adequate food and lodging. We lived peacefully in the village nearby Topoľčany till about mid-July 1945. By then it appeared that the country was adequately stabilized to travel to Košice. The adults decided that my mother and Karči would set out for Košice, and Manci would stay with me. I think that this arrangement was governed by the fact that Manci was not well.

During my mother's absence my activities were essentially unregulated. I could do more or less what I wanted. Behind the houses on the outskirts of Topoľčany was a large mountain that was mined for some type of minerals. A narrow gauge railway led to the top of the mountain. A small locomotive lay turned over on its side near the tracks, but the train of wagons that were the size of a wheelbarrow were intact on the tracks. Each wagon was the right size to hold one or two boys. Together with a group of boys, some my age, some little older, I engaged in what I now think was a very dangerous game. With a lot of effort we pushed the wagons to the top of the mountain where there was the barricaded entrance to the mine. The rear wagon had a brake that was activated by turning a wheel that applied a brake shoe to the wagon wheels. An older boy was usually in charge of the brake. Once we had pushed the train of little cars to the top, we piled into the cars and the brake was released. The train rolled down the hill gathering speed. The exhilarating ride took about ten minutes. With good luck on our side, we made it to the bottom of the hill safely every time.

While my mother and Karči were away, a typhoid fever epidemic broke out in our village, as well as in other villages around Topoľčany. In these villages water was obtained from wells and in our case also from a stream that ran at the edge of the village. The water became contaminated by typhoid fever, causing bacteria, most likely generated in corpses of people and animals buried in shallow graves. The bacteria from the infected decaying corpses seeped into the ground water contaminating wells and streams. The farmer from whom we rented the house came down with the infection, as did many other people in the village. A health system was quickly improvised and mobilized. People from the local government came to inspect the village. The order was given for all water to be boiled and buckets containing lime were placed in the outhouses. Every time we used the outhouse, we were required to pour a small cupful of lime into the outhouse hole.

During this time there was a shortage of workers in the village. Many of the men had not yet returned from the army or prisoner-of-war camps. With the farmer sick, his mother was recruited to take care of his herd of goats. She asked me to help her. Together we herded the goats into the pasture and my job was to keep the goats from straying into a field of clover. She told me that if goats ate clover, they would bloat and their intestines might explode. One day, the farmer's mother had to do some chores and left me fully in charge of the herd. Soon after she left, the goats ran into the clover field and started to feed on the clover. I ran around in panic, chasing the goats out of the clover field. By the time the farmer's mother returned, all the goats were out of the clover field peacefully eating regular grass. I did not mention the clover incident, but I was really worried. I kept waking up during the night fearing that I might hear goats exploding. First thing in the morning I ran to the barn to see the goats; They were all healthy and unharmed.

Some days later, we herded the goats into another field bordering a small creek. The farmer's mother was complaining how much work it was to boil all the water we were using, even water for washing. She claimed all this boiling was unnecessary. Pointing at the flowing creek, she said, that all we had to do was to look at the flowing water, and count the rocks over which the water flowed. The water would be perfectly fine after it flowed over seven large rocks. But she grumbled that she was forbidden to use her method of water purification. After a few weeks, the danger of typhoid fever passed. A few people in the village died, but most, including the farmer with whom we lived, recovered.

The summer went by. We measured the progress of time by the increasing height of the corn in the field. Toward the end of August my mother and Karči returned. By then we all knew that many of the Jews of Slovakia had been murdered, but it took several months to know the full extent of the killing. Eventually, the census showed that of the approximately 90,000 Jews that lived in Slovakia before the war, 70,000 were killed. Many Jews after surviving the camps – depleted and weakened – died of typhoid fever and other infections. My mother and Karči brought back the good news that Ernő and Erzsi survived and were back in Košice. Their survival was due to the fortunate coincidence of having found each other shortly after liberation of the concentration camp. The fate of other members of the family was not yet known.

Now that my mother and Karči had returned and reported that some of our relatives and family friends had survived and were in Košice, it was time for us to go there. Trains, while not on a regular schedule, had started to run again and it appeared to be possible to get back to Košice relatively easily. At the beginning of September we set off for Košice – a long trip, with endless waiting for train connections.

Back in Košice

Most of the surviving Jews from the eastern part of Slovakia gravitated to Košice, and now all the surviving members of our family were there. Somehow, everybody found temporary accommodations. My mother and I moved in with Ernő who was able to reclaim his house with most of the furniture intact. Manci and Karči rented an apartment just off the Košice main street. Jewish life gradually reopened in Košice.

Some of the pre-war Jewish buildings were repaired and one of the three Košice synagogues was reopened for regular services. A reception center was opened with its main role to serve as a temporary station for returning survivors. The survivors straggled in, and here they could get food and a bed to sleep. I knew that my father Ignac was dead, killed in the outskirts of Banska Bystrica. But somehow, I felt that if I kept looking for him, I might find him. Every morning, I walked to the reception center, looked at the bulletin board where messages were posted, went to the dining room where I walked from table to table showing people a photo of my father and asked the newcomers if they had seen him. They looked at the photo and shook their heads. At the beginning, my mother told me that there was no use to my inquiry, because my father had been killed. After a few days, however, she just let me continue doing what I started. After a few weeks the arrival of survivors slowed down, and then stopped. The reception center closed.

The survivors had to bear heart-breaking losses. Ernő's wife Bőzsi and son Gyuri had been killed. Erzsi and her husband Geza survived, but their daughter Klari was killed. Klara, the woman who cofounded the Jewish orphanage in Košice, returned to learn that her two sons and husband were murdered. From my birth father's immediate family I was the only one who survived. My grandparents, my aunt, my uncles, and all my cousins were murdered.

Almost every Jew that survived had to cope with the destruction of his or her family through death of a husband, wife, or children. The nearly unbearable devastation and loneliness seemed to have evoked a drive to resume their lives as rapidly as possible. For most people this entailed reconstituting a family. Most of the survivors knew each other, or at least each other's families. Therefore, finding new marriage partners, mostly by recommendation, went relatively quickly and smoothly. Within two or three months of arriving in Košice, my mother had three suitors. Korach Lajcsi was the first, the pharmacist who had been married to my birth-father's sister whom I had visited in Hust with my grandparents. His wife and three sons had been killed. The second suitor was a relatively well-known violinist who played with the Košice symphony orchestra. His wife and several children had been killed. Another suitor was Gasper Klenko, a successful businessman whose wife and daughter had been killed. I had spent time with each of them and my mother selected Gasper to be her new husband.

My uncle Ernő married Eva Braun, whose husband had committed suicide in the early days of the war. Eva was the younger sister of Klara who married Jenci Weinberger, a watchmaker from Humenne. His wife and two children had also been killed. My mother knew him and his family and recommended him to Klara.

Topoľčany Pogrom

Shortly after we left Topoľčany, an event occurred in Slovakia that altered the fate of Slovakian Jews. Records indicate that Jewish merchants lived in Topoľčany at least on a temporary basis as early as the 1300s. In 1649, a few Jewish families were allowed to settle permanently in Topoľčany. With some ups and downs, the community grew and by the late 1700s about 200 Jews lived there. Around that time a fully fledged Jewish community was formed with its own synagogue, rabbi, schools, and cemetery.

At the outbreak of WWII, about 3,000 of the total Topoľčany population of 12,000 were Jews. According to the census, they owned 320 of the 615 registered businesses (52%). About 70% of physicians and 57% of lawyers were Jews. Jews actively participated in the social and political life of the town. The occupational distributions were similar in other Slovak towns.

Prior to WWII, relations between Jews and their Gentile neighbors were cordial and often actually friendly. But as the deportation of Jews began, greed took over the behavior of many. The opportunity to take over Jewish businesses and usurp possessions of the Jews was too tempting for many to resist.

Of the 3,000 Topoľčany Jews, about 500 survived the Holocaust. Most of them returned to Topoľčany to restart their lives. The survivors asked for the return of their illegally expropriated properties. This demand triggered a wave of antisemitism that culminated on September 24, 1945, a few weeks after most of the surviving Jews had returned. On that day, a Jewish physician at the request of the town health department, was vaccinating children at the local school. A rumor was started that he was poisoning the children. A mob of about 300 people attacked the Jews. Forty-seven Jews were injured, while 15 had to be hospitalized. The police did very little to stop the rampage. The rest of the gentile population likewise stood by passively.

Such violence against Jews occurred in many other Slovak towns. Altogether, throughout Slovakia, in such post-Holocaust attacks, more than 36 Jews were killed and many more were injured. While only a small fraction of the population actively participated in the post-war violence against the Jews, with some notable exceptions, most stood by passively without attempting to alter the course of events.

My own experience confirms this observation. In 1945, I was enrolled in a Košice public school in the age-appropriate fifth grade. Only a small number of young people my age survived the war. The Košice middle school had about 15 Jewish students. In the playground and on the way home we were frequently accosted by the gentile students. They shoved us, threw stones at us and subjected us to traditional antisemitic invectives. Some of us complained to the teachers, but they ignored the situation.

I was involved in several fights and got my face smashed with a rock twice, both times resulting in a black eye. Each time, my mother rushed me to a second cousin who was an ophthalmologist. He examined me carefully and reassured us that no permanent damage was done.

The Israeli Zionist youth movements sent emissaries to recruit and organize the surviving youth for subsequent emigration to Israel. Youth movements representing the spectrum of Israeli politics, from socialist to ultra-Orthodox, came to Košice. I joined *Hashomer Hatzair*, a movement with a strongly left-leaning ideology, focused on the task to have its members join Kibbutzim affiliated with *Mapam*, an Israeli Labor Zionist political party. This youth movement had a strong formative influence on me. It informed many of my major decisions, including whom I would later marry.

In addition to their political mission, the Israeli Zionist emissaries also taught us how to fight, and that made a difference. They showed us how to fight with sticks and taught us how to make and shoot slingshots. In one of the encounters with a relatively large group of boys, we shot back stones with our new slingshots. Our adversaries suddenly started to run away. We learned that one of the boys was hit in the eye with a stone and had to be taken to the hospital. It was rumored that he was blinded in that eye. Our ability and willingness to fight back greatly reduced the incidents of bullying.

The leadership of the youth movements organized three-week summer camps for their members which I attended in 1946 and 1947. The summer camp was set up in the mountains of the Czech part of Czechoslovakia on a large meadow with a brook running along its edge. The nearest town was about 10 miles away. Our campsite was accessible from the town by a narrow unpaved road. The camp setup was primitive bare-bone basic. We campers were each given an army surplus ground sheet. Two sheets could be buttoned together and with support poles and rope could be set up to form a somewhat leaky pup tent. Two of us shared the tent. We dug latrines and used the water in the brook for washing. My tent mate was a boy named Schneider whose hygiene was less than adequate even by my youthful standards. He seemed to never have washed and – as time went on – smelled more and more pungent.

As I see it now, the camp was a very important experience for us. For the past few years, we children have had very limited interactions with people our age. Most of us had been either in hiding or running from danger using false identities. Here in the camp, we had the opportunity to play, sing, do art projects, learn scouting skills – activities normal for children our age.

My first experience of summer camp was at times uncomfortable and difficult, but on the whole it proceeded as planned. The following year, camping went differently. During the second week of the camp, I was woken up by someone violently shaking our tent and yelling to get out quickly, pack our stuff immediately and leave. The nights were cold, so except for taking off our shoes we mostly slept fully dressed. I jumped out of my sleeping bag and looked out of the tent. Our camping field was filling up with soldiers arriving by trucks, and armored vehicles. They were positioned around the field hidden by trees and bushes. A contingent of soldiers was tossing our belongings and gear helter-skelter onto the back of the trucks and we were ordered to climb on quickly. I heard someone shout that Bandera's army would be here any minute. As the trucks turned around, and drove us out of our campground we heard gun fire and explosions coming behind us.

Later, I learned the details of what had happened that night. In the summer of 1941 when Germany invaded the Soviet Union, Ukraine was very quickly overrun. Soon after, long suppressed Ukrainian nationalist movements reemerged with the purpose of establishing an ethnically pure Ukrainian state with one language and one people. The nationalist movements formed a united front and organized the Ukrainian National Army. Its initial strength was estimated at 200,000 soldiers. The newly formed Ukrainian army allied itself with Germany and formulated three goals: fight the Soviet Union, rid Ukraine of its Polish populations and eliminate its Jewish population. They were responsible for murdering many Poles and Jews.

As the war progressed and it became evident that Germany would lose the war, many abandoned the Ukrainian National Army, but several thousand remained trapped behind the Soviet army lines. They knew that if they fell into the hands of the Soviet army they would be immediately executed. They organized into partisan groups and started to make their way toward US-occupied Germany. Occasionally, their progress was halted by skirmishes with local army units that discovered their escape route. The Ukrainian unit that was intercepted at the site of our summer camp was under the leadership of Stepan Bandera, one of the most prominent Ukrainian fascist leaders and Nazi collaborators. In these skirmishes some Ukrainian soldiers were killed but most escaped. Once the Ukrainians reached the American sector they were usually granted asylum, and emigrated most often to the US or Canada. These skirmishes with escaping Ukrainian fascist troops continued till about 1950, well after WWII ended. Stepan Bandera who headed for our camp successfully made it to the West, and was assassinated in 1959 in Munich, presumably by the NKVD.

Leaving Europe

As time went on, it became increasingly evident that Slovakia remained a hostile environment for Jews, and any attempt to live a normal life there was futile. Acquaintances and family were leaving Czechoslovakia daily. The youth movements in Košice disbanded, because not enough young people remained to maintain activities.

Ernő, Eve, Klara and Jenci were the first in our immediate family to emigrate. In 1947, they left Slovakia (then Czechoslovakia) to settle in Toronto, Canada. Eva and Klara's older brother had emigrated to Canada before the war and was now well established in Toronto. He promised to help them in their transition.

My new father, Gasper, was reluctant to leave Czechoslovakia. He had restarted his wholesale clothing business and financially was doing very well. At this point he was already 52 years old and felt he was too old to start all over again in a country where he had no business connections and the language and customs were foreign to him. My mother, of course, was committed to him, but I was adamant about leaving Slovakia with or without my parents. My independent emigration was a possibility, because soon after the State of Israel was established the Israeli government initiated a program called "Youth Aliah", designed to bring European youth to Israel. At the age of 13, I was able to obtain my own passport and register for the Youth Aliah program.

On February 1948, the Communist party – at that time a minority party – engineered a coup d'état and took over the Czechoslovak government. Very quickly the Communist party instituted a dictatorship that took control of all aspects of life. The borders were closed and emigration from Czechoslovakia was prohibited. Rudolf Slansky, the Jewish Secretary of the Communist party, intervened on behalf of the Jews, making the argument that persistent antisemitism would be an ongoing problem for the country. He prevailed, and Jews were allowed to emigrate.

Around this time, an event in my school reinforced my resolve to leave Czechoslovakia. I formed friendships with a few non-Jewish students and six of us in my class – three boys and three girls – had formed a small club. We talked about books we read, and occasionally, on a Sunday, we went hiking or went to watch a movie. On a Friday afternoon, in the spring of 1949, an announcement was made on the speakers that were installed in every classroom, that there would be a demonstration and march in support of the Communist Party on Sunday. All the students were to show up at the town central square to hear the speeches by party executives and then participate in the march up the main street. Small red Party flags would be distributed prior to the march. Our little group decided to skip the demonstration and go on our previously planned hike. We certainly did not expect that our absence would be noticed. However, someone was watching, and denounced us.

The following Monday morning, another message came through the speakers announcing that several students did not come to the demonstration. This is a serious breach of proletarian solidarity that has consequences, the voice from the speaker declared. It was announced that the afternoon classes of the following day would be cancelled and the whole student body would assemble in the auditorium to discuss the issue.

That next afternoon in front of all the assembled students, the school principal named the six of us, and denounced us as the antisocial elements in the community. Such behavior was unacceptable and would not be tolerated. Several students were called up to the podium and continued the barrage of denunciations. The meeting ended with the principal once again taking the microphone and telling the six of us to write a letter of apology. The assembly was then dismissed, and afternoon classes resumed. After class my home teacher asked to speak to me. He told me that this was a serious matter, and my behavior has been entered into my record. Unless I redeemed myself, I would never be allowed to enter a university.

Finally, my parents understood that I was prepared to leave without them, and they agreed to leave Czechoslovakia. They obtained for all three of us exit visas from Czechoslovakia and entry permits to enter Canada. They bought train tickets to Cuxhaven, a sea port near Hamburg, from where we were scheduled to sail on the SS Samaria to Quebec, Canada.

We could take with us very little – no jewelry except wedding rings, only $100 per person and a suitcase of clothing and other personal belongings. We each had to prepare a list of items we planned to take with us and submit the list to the customs police. On the eve of our departure, in mid-October 1949, the customs officials came to our apartment and supervised our packing the suitcases. Then they sealed each suitcase with an official tape. We were now all set to leave Czechoslovakia and Europe.

The parting was difficult as my mother was very attached to her sisters, and Erzsi, her husband and two sons born after the war, had decided to remain in Košice, as did Manci and Karči. For them the uprooting and moving to a strange land was too daunting. Still, most Jews saw that there was no future in Slovakia and by the end of 1949 about 90% of the surviving Jews had emigrated, mainly to Israel, Canada, the US and Australia. Currently, only about 2,000 Jews remain in Slovakia.

The following morning, we took the train to Prague, and after staying overnight in a hotel, in the morning we boarded the train for Germany. We arrived in Hamburg in the evening of the same day, and again stayed overnight in a nearby, recently reconstructed, hotel. The next day we took a local train to Cuxhaven, a ride of only about two-and-a-half hours.

Throughout our long trip across Germany, we passed several large cities such as Frankfurt and Cologne. I had seen bombed-out buildings in Slovakia, but nothing close to the sights we saw from the passing train. These German cities were totally devastated, reduced to rubble. We saw one exception. In the midst of destruction, the huge Gothic cathedral in Cologne was blackened by fire, but had remained standing; The only upright building in the midst of a totally destroyed city. Subsequently, I read that the cathedral was saved from being bombed, because – as the most prominent and recognizable structure – it was used for orienting allied pilots on their bombing missions. Considering the devastation I saw in 1949, I was amazed at the state of the country when I went to Germany in the mid-1980s to attend a conference. The cities were flawlessly repaired. The old medieval city centers were restored – often, stone by stone – to their former appearance.

The Cologne Cathedral (Public Domain).

In Cuxhaven my mother, father and I joined a long line of passengers boarding the RMS Samaria. The line moved quickly and soon we were on the top deck of the ship where a steward directed us to go down two flights into the depth of the ship. Here two long dormitory rooms – one for men, the other for women – were our lodging for the voyage. We were each assigned a narrow bed with a pillow and a thin blanket. We must have been close to the steam engines, because the space was noisy and the beds shook. Gaspar was very upset. He paid for and seemingly reserved a private cabin on the top deck of the ship, and here we were in near-steerage conditions. We had clearly been cheated.

Gaspar wanted to speak to the ship's bursar to see what could be done about changing our accommodations. He and I went to the top deck where we saw the bursar sitting behind a desk talking to passengers who came to him with one problem or another. What impressed me most about the bursar was his linguistic ability. In the short period of a few minutes he spoke Hungarian, Polish, Italian and some other languages I did not even recognize. Gaspar spoke to him in German explaining our predicament. The bursar looked at our tickets and confirmed that we had been cheated. We were charged for a private cabin and issued dormitory accommodations, but at this point nothing could be done; the ship was totally full. We were lucky, however, he said. Some people were sold counterfeit tickets and had been denied passage altogether.

My first view of the ocean – or so I thought – was from the deck of RMS Samaria in Cuxhaven that afternoon. I remember thinking that this was just another body of water much like one of the large lakes I had seen in Slovakia. I did not know that in reality, the Cuxhaven port was a well-sheltered harbor.

Toward evening, the ship pulled out of the harbor, and sailing through the night it brought us into the open Atlantic Ocean. And here is where I began to get the feel of the ocean. We were heading into a very intense Atlantic storm. Each day the storm was wilder, the waves higher. Most of the passengers were seasick as was I. After three days of seasickness, my nausea subsided and I was able to go up to the top deck. The waves were now so high that the stern of the ship came out of the water exposing the ship's propellers. The 1920s ship creaked and moaned loudly, sounding ominous. Throughout the day, the ship stopped from time to time to wait out the worst of the storm. Finally, the storm subsided, and after a 14-day voyage we sailed smoothly into Quebec harbor in the morning. The immigration card attached to my passport states that we arrived on October 25, 1949.

That same day we boarded the train for Toronto. In the late afternoon when the train pulled in, my uncle Ernő, Eva and her brother Karcsi were waiting for us in the arrival room. Karcsi had a large bright-blue Buick that I still remember clearly. He drove us to an apartment that Ernő had rented for us. We were now in Canada.

Shortly after we arrived in Canada we heard news from Czechoslovakia. Slansky lost his high political post, was arrested and the emigration of Jews was halted. Slansky together with 10 other high-ranking Jewish party members was tried on trumped-up, blatantly antisemitic charges. They were all found guilty, and most of them – including Slansky – were executed in 1952.

12

IN CANADA

When we arrived in Canada, Toronto was a sprawling city of about one million people. While it had many hallmarks of a large city – a great museum, a well-known university, excellent hospitals a good symphony orchestra – Toronto did not give the impression of a modern city. It did not have any significantly tall buildings, had no subway, lacked an opera house, and was subject to a range of highly restrictive "blue laws". Most strikingly, its telephone system was not automated. To make a telephone call you had to lift the receiver and tell the responding operator the phone number you wanted to reach. Party lines were common. This aspect of the telephone system stood out for me, because I was aware that the telephone system in Košice, a city much smaller than Toronto was fully automated. Most significantly for us newcomers, the city had very few apartment buildings, resulting in a severe shortage of affordable rentals. The solution to the housing problem was simple and helpful.

Most of the houses in the inner part of the city were single-family homes built in the early 1920s. Many of the owners converted these houses to two family dwellings. The conversion was simple and inexpensive. In one of the second-floor bedrooms, a sink, a refrigerator and a gas stove were installed, providing a kitchen for a makeshift second apartment. The owner-family occupied the ground and third floors while the second floor was rented out. The single bathroom which was on the second floor was shared by both families. All the families I knew who immigrated to Toronto initially settled into such an arrangement. Most, including my family, lived in such shared dwelling for five years or so, saved money, and then bought their own house that they rented in a similar arrangement. Many owners and renter families became friends and remained in life-long contact.

Several of my relatives and close acquaintances including Klara's nieces, Oli and Ilona, with their husbands, emigrated in the nick of time from Czechoslovakia to Toronto. The survivors from Eastern Slovakia who settled in Toronto formed a small, closed community. They provided help and emotional support to each other. They spoke almost exclusively Hungarian with each other, but they very quickly learned English. Most attended night classes in English as a second language, sponsored by the public school system, and read the local newspapers.

Canada was in the midst of a post-war boom with jobs and business opportunities readily available. Many of our acquaintances started small businesses in areas that were new to them, but were much needed in Toronto. Several became builders of new homes that were in great demand in post-war Canada. After a few difficult years, my uncle Ernő built a successful legal practice that advocated on behalf of surviving Jews. His focus was on obtaining restitution from Germany for seized properties and other damages inflicted by the Germans.

Gaspar first got a job in a factory making upholstered kitchen chrome chairs. He learned how to make them and how to organize their manufacture. Four months later he started a small, successful business of his own making such chrome chairs. My mother worked as a seamstress in a sweatshop making bed spreads. Within three years, she learned English well enough to become a sales person in a well-known Toronto department store. Within about 15 years they had saved enough money to retire. In the 1950s my parents, together with Ernő, Eva, Klara and Jenci, bought a six-plex and moved into three of the six apartments. Two of the other three were rented to relatives.

Family and friends in Toronto, early 1960s.

They lived together till the end of their lives. I took the group photograph in Toronto in the late 60s in the garden of their six-plex. The seated people are – starting on the right – my mother, Klara, Klara's husband Jenci, my third father Gaspar and Ernő's second wife Eva.

The adults had a ready-made social network. Every Sunday, they got together to play cards. They visited each other often, and talked frequently on the telephone. Occasionally during the summer, some of the families went on vacations together. My social situation was more difficult when we first arrived in Canada, also because I did not know any English. Very few young people my age survived the Holocaust, and none in my parents' circle of friends.

Clearly, learning English had to be my priority. Around November 1, close to my 14th birthday, I started attending a government-sponsored full-day English language program for newcomers. The class held in a neighborhood public school met from 9 am to 3 pm. I was the youngest person in the class. My classmates, about 30 of us, ranged in age from about 30 to 60 years. We came from all over Europe: Hungary, Ukraine, Germany, Sweden. The teacher was a young good-humored woman who taught us mostly by presenting presumably useful sentences such as: "How much does this bottle of milk cost?" She had a stack of pictures that illustrated the meaning of the words. We then repeated the words and finally the whole sentence over and over again. I made a list of the new words we used, about 20 each day, and tried to learn them. At first, I was very discouraged. I had read somewhere that there were 300,000 words in the English language. With that many words to learn, it would take me several decades to speak the language. Using a dictionary, I formulated a question I asked our English language teacher: "How many words do I need to know to begin understanding English?" She gave the very encouraging answer that only about 2,000 words would do it. That was certainly manageable and I redoubled my effort. After a month or so into my English studies, I went to the library and borrowed children's books with stories that I had already known, such as Little Red Riding hood, Snow White and the Seven Dwarfs, Ali Baba and the Forty Thieves, and started to read them. It was very helpful in my learning, as well as fun, to know the story well and be able to fill in gaps in my understanding of the language.

I also discovered a way to practice speaking English and here the rather primitive telephone system was useful. When I picked up the phone, an operator – always a woman – would answer with: "How may I connect you?" I would then ask, as an example, to be connected with Alhambra, a nearby movie house. After a few clicking sounds the Alhambra box-office attendant would answer the phone. I would then ask some question about the motion picture they were showing. As my English improved, my questions became more complex.

I was still lonely and spent much of my time walking the streets in the neighborhoods around Manning Street where we now lived. While walking I would glance at my word list and memorize my words for the day. One afternoon toward the end of December, while walking in the neighborhood, on Beatrice Street – where I had not walked before – I saw a painted sign hanging from the balcony of a house: *Hashomer Hatzair* (the same Socialist Zionist youth movement I had belonged to in Košice.)[1] The building was in darkness. I walked up the few steps leading to the front door, but it was locked.

The following day I returned, this time in the late afternoon. Lights were on in the building and the door was open. About half a dozen people in their late teens or early twenties were in the midst of some lively meeting in one of the downstairs rooms. When I walked in, they stopped talking and looked at me quizzically. In my broken English I told them that I had recently come to Canada from Czechoslovakia where I had belonged to Hashomer Hatzair. One of the group came over to me, introduced himself as Natan and told me that he was the leader of a group of boys my age and in fact one of them was also from Czechoslovakia. They met Friday and Saturday evenings and I should come back then. I returned the following Friday evening and joined a group of seven boys my age. A corresponding girls group was meeting in a room down the hall. That evening the group was learning about Darwinian evolution. The boys interrupted the discussion frequently with questions many of which I understood. After about an hour-long discussion, we joined the girls group in a larger space. Here we sang some folk songs and Hebrew songs that were familiar to me. We then did some folk dancing. The evening ended with the group going to a nearby diner for ice cream. Finding this familiar organization, within walking distance from my home, had a profound effect on my life. I now had a social and ideological focus in my life.

By mid-January, my language skills were adequate enough to be enrolled in grade eight of the neighborhood public school. Grade eight was an important transitional year in the Ontario school system. This was the last year of middle school after which students went on to high school. At that time, Ontario high school had a three-pronged system. Students, boys and girls, who were academically inclined and were likely to go on to college, were directed to a collegiate high school. Boys deemed less likely to go to college were transitioned to a technical high school. Girls in the same category went on to a commercial high school. While it was possible for a student on a given track to switch to another track, it took some effort, and as far as I saw, this seldom happened. I was placed on the collegiate track. I don't know the basis for that decision since my middle school teachers had known me only for about three months when that decision was made, and during that time I had not provided much data about my academic abilities. I think one event may have been decisive. The class was about to start a unit on music appreciation, and Mr. Parker, our home teacher, started to play some music on the record player that I immediately recognized. He asked the class if anyone knew what that piece was. I was the only one to raise his hand. The teacher called on me and I answered. "This is *Eine Kleine Nacht Musik* by Wolfgang Amadeus Mozart." The students giggled but stopped when Mr. Parker confirmed my answer. He seemed impressed, and perhaps that affected his decision.

While I was in grade eight, I was certainly a foreign element in the school. I was socially ignored; no one reached out to me. One day, I was walking along College Street, one of the main streets running through our neighborhood, when I saw a sign in the window of a grocery store: "Help wanted at Economy Tea and Coffee inquire within". I had become aware of the possibility of school boys and girls earning money in Canada by taking on part-time jobs. At that time this opportunity did not exist in Slovakia. I talked to the grocery storekeeper who directed me to the back door that lead to a large room where I met Art Greenberg, the owner of Economy Tea and Coffee. This was a small enterprise. They received coffee beans in 50-pound burlap bags and tea in large plywood boxes. Art usually roasted the coffee and the roasted coffee beans were packaged into one-pound bags. Fred, that is how I remember his name, currently the only other employee, delivered the one-pound bags of coffee and tea to restaurants, diners and luncheonettes all over Toronto.

He needed someone for about two hours a day to weigh and package the coffee and tea. On the spot he decided that I could have the job if I wanted it. I don't remember how much he was going to pay me. I think it was about 50 cents an hour. I started work the following day from 4 to 6 in the afternoon. The following day, I came to work and met Fred. He was a tall lanky young man with a front tooth missing. We talked a bit and he told me how much he liked Art and what a decent person he was. Art had an eleven-year-old daughter who was not able to walk, Fred thought she had had polio that left her paralyzed. Art loved her with total dedication.

I liked working at Economy Tea and Coffee, in particularly watching the process of roasting the coffee beans. The main roasting apparatus was a large rotating drum perforated by evenly spaced holes. Art lit the gas burners under the bottom of the drum and tilted the drum with insulated gloves on his hands. He then poured the 50-pound sack of raw coffee beans into the drum and set the drum rotating by pushing a button on the panel attached to the wall. He liked explaining the process to me. Periodically, he stopped the drum for a few seconds, reached in with a spoon, took out some beans, looked at them, inhaled their aroma and either declared the roasting done or continued the roasting. He explained that roasting takes about 20 minutes but it is not possible to set a precise time for roasting even if you know the exact temperature in the roaster. That time depends somewhat on the size of the beans, where they were grown, and how they were harvested. This is where the skill of the person testing the state of the roasted bean comes in. After the coffee beans are deemed adequately roasted, the gas flame is turned off, the drum is pulled out and the hot roasted beans are doused with cold water from a watering can. This generates a cloud of steam with the pleasing aroma of roasted coffee.

I worked at Economy Tea and Coffee for about a year until the owner of the front store, from whom Art rented the backroom space, gave notice that he needed the space for his own expansion and would not be renewing Art's lease. Art told Fred and me about this development and added that business has not been good. Therefore, he would not reopen and we would have to find new jobs. Jobs were plentiful however, and the following day I was hired to stock shelves in the neighborhood branch of Dominion store, a large grocery chain store. The job was for Saturdays, 8am to 6pm, with half an hour off for lunch.

High school

My transition to high school went smoothly. By the time the school year began, my command of English was fully adequate. The high school curriculum was essentially classical. All students were enrolled in Latin and French, while ancient Greek was also an option. We studied ancient Greek and Roman history, modern European and Canadian history, Algebra and Geometry were also part of the curriculum, and of course English Literature and composition. We learned very little science; some biology, but as I recall, no Physics or Chemistry.

This was a difficult time of my life. I was clearly still a foreigner in this country with accented English and ignorant of many prevalent customs. I was about 16 years old and boys and girls in my class already began to date, go to dances and movies together. I was way too insecure to initiate such connections. I was anxious, uncertain how to fit into this new world. Around this time, I developed physical stress-induced symptoms. I had heart burn almost every night and most disturbingly severe insomnia. The sofa in the living room was my bed and I tossed and turned most of the night. Sodium bicarbonate always relieved the heart burn, but the insomnia seemed intractable. I finally told my mother about my problem. Somehow, she always knew when I could not sleep. She would come sit near my bed, hold my hand till I fell asleep. Within a few weeks my insomnia was gone.

My dissatisfaction with the curriculum was growing. I could not see how much of anything I was learning would be of use to me. This perspective was brought to a clear focus for me in my third year of high school during a class on Canadian history. The historical event being taught was the Upper Canada (now Ontario) Uprising. As presented by the teacher, the uprising peaked on December 5th, 1837, when some 100 men marched up Young Street to the English-appointed Lieutenant Governor's mansion, and demanded greater independence for Upper Canada. Apparently, a song had been composed highlighting this event. In an attempt to bring the event to life, the teacher raised his foot, put it on his chair and started to sing the song. The class looked at him with some surprise. He sang for a minute or so and then while singing, he lowered his foot attempting to place it back on the ground but instead his foot went into the waste paper basket next to the chair. While still singing, he tried to pull his foot out of the basket. The foot however, was firmly wedged in the basket and bounced up and down clanging on the floor as he raised and lowered his foot. The class giggled and laughed, but I, as I now understand it, had a panic attack. This type of learning would certainly not help me survive in a world I was likely to face. Here I was in a still-strange land. The Korean War was raging, with both

Canada and the US deeply involved. The nuclear confrontation between the Soviet Union and the US was an increasing possibility, and I was totally unprepared for the looming crisis. I had no skills or relevant knowledge. I knew nuclear weapons existed, and threatened the survival of the world, but knew nothing of their operation. I knew nothing about the structure or functioning of the world I lived in. I didn't even know how a car worked. And here I was studying the Upper Canada Uprising, an event of very little consequence, and no help in dealing with looming crisis. This was an epiphanic moment for me. With a sudden urgency I realized that I had to gain an understanding of how the world functioned in order to survive.

It was at this point that I decided to study science and engineering and focus my attention on learning to master some technical skills. That afternoon, I phoned Natan, the leader of our youth group in Hashomer Hatzair. He had quit university and was now working in a machine shop, preparing to join a kibbutz in Israel. I asked him if he would teach me how to run some of the equipment in his machine shop. He readily agreed, and told me to come to the machine shop the next day after his work hours. When I arrived, we were the only two in the machine shop. Over the next few days, he taught me the rudiments of using a drill, a lathe, and a milling machine. And over the next few weeks I practiced by making various decorations, brooches, candle sticks, and vases. I gave some to my mother and to girls I liked. They were fun to make and fun to give.

As part of my resolve to expand my knowledge and skill base, I looked into the extracurricular activities in my high school. A variety of club activities were offered: chess, debating, drama, performance music, and the rifle club organized under the auspices of the Royal Canadian Cadets.

The main focus of the rifle club was participation in shooting competitions involving local high school clubs. I joined the rifle club, thinking that learning how to use and handle a rifle could be useful in gaining some agency. The rifle club met only sporadically to practice target shooting before these competitions. That suited me well, because I was very busy with school work, my new job, and my growing involvement with the Zionist youth movement, Hashomer Hatzair, that provided a reliable anchor and base for me in this still foreign country.

The aim of Hashomer Hatzair (or the 'movement'), was to motivate Jewish youth to immigrate to Israel and to join a kibbutz associated with Hashomer Hatzair. Working toward this goal the movement provided a great way for young people to grow and pass through the teenage years. Recruitment for the movement began with children aged 11 and older. Members moved from age groups to age group. At about the age of 17 members became leaders of younger groups. Activities were centered on involvement in scouting-type activities, in cultural activities, and in increasing political indoctrination. At a very low, or no cost, the movement provided opportunity for members to attend summer, and most years also winter camp. The movement had branches in several large cities in US and Canada. During school vacations we often traveled to these cities for joint activities, or at times just to reconnect with friends. In the 1950s, when I belonged to Hashomer Hatzair, hitchhiking was a safe, inexpensive, adventure and a convenient way for young people to travel. This carefree life of youth came to an end, when at the age of 21 or so we were expected to immigrate to Israel and join a kibbutz.

I met Judith Taplitz, my future wife, who was a member of the Movement in New York City. Most young people in

Hashomer Hatzair, likewise found their future partners in the movement. Although I remained an active member, the goal of the movement diverged from my resolve to focus on studying science. In 1956, Judith and I left the movement, got married and moved to New York City. In 1960, I received my undergraduate degree in Electrical Engineering from Columbia University and in the fall of that year I was accepted and enrolled in a joint graduate program in Electrical Engineering and Physics also at Columbia University. In 1964, I completed my Ph.D. work in that field. My thesis work was very successful, and it launched my career in teaching and research.

I stayed on at Columbia University for another year as a researcher, completing some of the experiments I started during my thesis work. I was also appointed an instructor teaching graduate engineering courses. Following my year at Columbia, I joined the faculty at Yale University where I stayed for nine years. I was then offered a faculty position at Boston College where I worked for 46 years. After teaching and doing research for 56 years in a variety of fields including quantum devices, medical physics, atmospheric chemistry, and climate change, I retired from academia on June 30, 2020.

EPILOGUE

As I think about the events described in this memoir, I continue to be amazed by my mother's intelligence, judgement, and resilience that made it possible for us to survive those dark and dangerous times. Here was a young woman who grew up in a small, albeit modern, Jewish community in a small town, Humenne, in eastern Slovakia, within a closed circle of friends, and with very limited contact outside her narrow world. After she married, she moved to a yet smaller town, and became a part of her husband's family and circle of friends, becoming perhaps even more sheltered. Before WWII, the largest city she visited was Košice, itself not a major metropolis, where her brother and sister lived. She never stayed there for more than a few days at a time. Yet in the spring of 1944, when the final and total elimination of Jews in Slovakia was initiated and ruthlessly implemented, she knew exactly what to do, each step of the way, and did it brilliantly.

When necessary, she had to assume the persona of a young peasant girl from a small Slovak village, Anna Hritzakova, whose forged Arian papers she was using. Our survival depended on her assuming this role convincingly. This was essential, for example, when we were stopped by a policeman at the railroad station, and asked for identification papers, or when she applied for a job, or looked for a place for us to live. Later, after the war, when I asked her how she accomplished this, she explained that when Anna was a maid in our household for several years, she, my mother, had intuitively learned to copy her mannerisms. When Anna drank tea or coffee from a cup that was on a saucer, she never lifted the cup off the saucer. Always, holding the cup in one hand, the saucer in the other, she raised both of them, and drank from the cup with it on the saucer. Anna never ate holding a fork in one hand and knife in the other. She first cut the food, put the knife down, and then ate using only the fork. Anna never sat with her legs crossed. When sitting, each foot was firmly planted on the ground. Anna spoke with a regional Zemplin accent, distinctly different from the accent taught in schools, and used by most people in urban centers. When required, my mother was able to switch into Anna's behavior patterns seamlessly.

The psychological strain on my mother during our year on false papers must have been enormous: isolation, life-threatening situations, loneliness, particularly after the capture of my father Ignac. We had no idea what happened to any of our family. Everyone we met was a stranger, and everyone could potentially expose us as Jews, causing our deportation and certain death. And my mother was able to bear this situation with its dangers its uncertainties, and function through it all.

Then the war suddenly ended and my mother could again retrieve her own identity. But the world she had known was now totally shattered. I think that my survival helped her to adjust to the new reality of her life. She took great pleasure in my professional and personal successes. She loved my wife Judith, and especially doted on our children Michael and Deborah. We visited her in Toronto, and several times a year she visited and spent time with us in Newton, a suburb of Boston. She developed a close and loving relationship with her grandchildren.

In 1971, she was diagnosed with lung cancer that turned out to be inoperable. We will never know the source of the disease. She was a non-smoker, but she did work for three years in a Toronto sweat shop sowing chanel bedspreads that filled the air with lint that she continually inhaled.

In the spring of 1975, my mother was in a Toronto hospital, close to death. Michael was 13 years old studying for his bar mitzvah. Deborah, five years younger, was eight. We traveled to Toronto, and at my mother's bedside Michael chanted his assigned portion from the Torah. This was an important and moving event for all of us. She died a few days later. Our children Michael and Deborah, now into their middle age, raising their own children, continue to speak and think of my mother often – with love and fond memories.

My mother with Michael and Deborah.

ACKNOWLEDGMENTS

I want to thank my wife Judith Taplitz and my son and daughter Michael and Deborah Davidovits for their very helpful discussions, comments and encouragement during the preparation of the manuscript.

I am indebted to Dalibor Danko for his interest in the history of Moldava, and for letting me use the image from his postcard collection.

I am thankful and moved by the work of the filmmaker Dušan Hudec for his documenting the fate of Jews in Slovakia and shedding light on the death of my father.

With great admiration and appreciation I thank Liesbeth Heenk, founder and Publisher of Amsterdam Publishers, who made the publication of this memoir possible.

NOTES

2. My Mother and her Sisters

1. https://www.youtube.com/watch?v=1IKjW3I_CvM
2. https://www.youtube.com/watch?v=9vjNdSOgFso

5. Humenne

1. This song is still sung in Slovakia and a recent very amateur version is uploaded on YouTube https://www.youtube.com/watch?v=DotGwazFToc .
2. The Catholic church was, by and large, silent in the midst of the Holocaust and did very little to help Jews in their awful predicament. Slovakia however, presented the Vatican with a unique situation. The president of Slovakia, Josef Tiso, was an ordained Roman Catholic priest and the prominent members of Tiso's Slovak fascist government were ardent Catholics. By mid-1942 the mass murder of deported Jews was widely known. The policy of mass murder of Jews by an essentially Catholic government in Slovakia was increasingly an embarrassment to the Vatican. Domenico Tardini, the Vatican Undersecretary of State wrote in a memorandum: "Everyone understands that the Holy See cannot stop Hitler. But who can understand that it does not know how to rein in a priest?" Tiso was threatened with serious sanctions if he did not stop deportations.

8. On the Run

1. The conversion is actually very simple. Wood is burned under low oxygen conditions, producing carbon monoxide and hydrogen gases. These gases are then compressed and injected into the cylinders of the engine where the gases are ignited under oxygen-rich conditions and then burn much the same way as gasoline vapors burn in a regular internal combustion engine.
2. In time of peace, at a high temperature of about 1000 degrees Celcius, calcium carbonate $CaCO_3$ (lime stone) was converted to calcium oxide (lime CaO), a material used in a wide range of industrial and agricultural applications.

9. Bratislava

1. In an interesting coincidence, last year I was watching a German TV series about a Berlin hospital, Charite, during World War II. As part of an episode a few minutes of a propaganda training film for the hospital physicians was shown. I immediately recognized the segment shown as part of the full-length German propaganda documentary we were exposed to that Sunday afternoon.
2. Turčianske Teplice means Turkish warm baths.

10. Rakša

1. The current website for Rakša does not mention the resort and simply states: "Rakša is a village and municipality in Turčianske Teplice District..." One can however still rent rooms in the renovated peasant houses for about 10 euros per night ($11).

12. In Canada

1. Hashomer Hatzair means Young Guard.

ABOUT THE AUTHOR

Paul Davidovits was born in 1935 in Moldava, a small town in Czechoslovakia (now Slovakia). His father died when Paul was not quite three years old. His mother and he then moved back to Humenne, his mother's home town. Two years later she re-married. They survived the Holocaust by using forged documents, and rapidly moving from town to town whenever anyone appeared to become suspicious of their identities.

By the time WWII ended, all of Paul's paternal family and most of his maternal family had been killed, including his mother's second husband. Paul's mother married the third time, and in 1949 the remnant of the family immigrated to Toronto, Canada. There Paul completed high school and a three-year program in Electrical Technology.

After working for a year in industry as an electrical technologist, Paul married, and he and his wife moved to New York City. Here Paul continued his education at Columbia University, receiving the B.S. (1960), M.S. (1961)

and Ph.D. (1964) degrees in a joint program in Physics and Electrical Engineering.

In 1964-1965 he was appointed at Columbia University as Research Associate in Physics and Lecturer in Electrical Engineering. In 1965 he joined the faculty at Yale University as Assistant Professor of Applied Science (1965-1970), and then as Associate Professor (1970-1974). In 1974 he accepted an appointment at Boston College as Professor of Chemistry, a position he retained for 46 years, teaching and conducting research in physical chemistry.

From 1994 to 1998 he was Chairman of the Boston College Chemistry Department. During his tenure at Boston College, he was also a consultant for 40 years at Aerodyne Research Inc. in Billerica MA, where together with Aerodyne scientists he studied the basic physico-chemical properties of gas-liquid interactions relevant to atmospheric chemistry and climate change.

After teaching and doing research for 56 years in a variety of fields, including quantum devices, chemical kinetics, medical physics, atmospheric chemistry, and climate change, Davidovits retired from academia on June 30, 2020 as Professor of Chemistry Emeritus. His scientific work is described in 170 publications he has authored or co-authored. He has written two textbooks (one of them currently in its 5th edition), and has co-edited a text on the alkali-halide vapors. He holds three patents.

He has received several awards for his work including, together with R. Minsky and D. Egger, the Year 2000, R.W. Wood Prize "for seminal contributions to confocal microscopy."

He has been married since 1957 and has two adult children. He is an avid hiker as well as a swimmer and a cyclist.

Dear Reader,

If you have enjoyed reading my book,
please do leave a review on Amazon or Goodreads.
A few kind words would be enough.
This would be greatly appreciated.

Alternatively, if you have read my book as Kindle eBook you could leave a rating.
That is just one simple click, indicating how many stars of five you think this book deserves.
This will only cost you a split second.
Thank you very much in advance!

Paul.

AMSTERDAM PUBLISHERS HOLOCAUST LIBRARY

The series **Holocaust Survivor Memoirs World War II** consists of the following autobiographies of survivors:

Outcry. Holocaust Memoirs, by Manny Steinberg

Hank Brodt Holocaust Memoirs. A Candle and a Promise, by Deborah Donnelly

The Dead Years. Holocaust Memoirs, by Joseph Schupack

Rescued from the Ashes. The Diary of Leokadia Schmidt, Survivor of the Warsaw Ghetto, by Leokadia Schmidt

My Lvov. Holocaust Memoir of a twelve-year-old Girl, by Janina Hescheles

Remembering Ravensbrück. From Holocaust to Healing, by Natalie Hess

Wolf. A Story of Hate, by Zeev Scheinwald with Ella Scheinwald

Save my Children. An Astonishing Tale of Survival and its Unlikely Hero, by Leon Kleiner with Edwin Stepp

Holocaust Memoirs of a Bergen-Belsen Survivor & Classmate of Anne Frank, by Nanette Blitz Konig

Defiant German - Defiant Jew. A Holocaust Memoir from inside the Third Reich, by Walter Leopold with Les Leopold

In a Land of Forest and Darkness. The Holocaust Story of two Jewish Partisans, by Sara Lustigman Omelinski

Holocaust Memories. Annihilation and Survival in Slovakia, by Paul Davidovits

From Auschwitz with Love. The Inspiring Memoir of Two Sisters' Survival, Devotion and Triumph Told by Manci Grunberger Beran & Ruth Grunberger Mermelstein, by Daniel Seymour

Remetz. Resistance Fighter and Survivor of the Warsaw Ghetto, by Jan Yohay Remetz

My March Through Hell. A Young Girl's Terrifying Journey to Survival, by Halina Kleiner with Edwin Stepp

Roman's Journey, by Roman Halter

Beyond Borders. Escaping the Holocaust and Fighting the Nazis. 1938-1948, by Rudi Haymann

The Engineers. A memoir of survival through World War II in Poland and Hungary, by Henry Reiss

Memoirs by Elmar Rivosh, Sculptor (1906-1967). Riga Ghetto and Beyond, by Elmar Rivosh

The series **Holocaust Survivor True Stories** consists of the following biographies:

Among the Reeds. The true story of how a family survived the Holocaust, by Tammy Bottner

A Holocaust Memoir of Love & Resilience. Mama's Survival from Lithuania to America, by Ettie Zilber

Living among the Dead. My Grandmother's Holocaust Survival Story of Love and Strength, by Adena Bernstein Astrowsky

Heart Songs. A Holocaust Memoir, by Barbara Gilford

Shoes of the Shoah. The Tomorrow of Yesterday, by Dorothy Pierce

Hidden in Berlin. A Holocaust Memoir, by Evelyn Joseph Grossman

Separated Together. The Incredible True WWII Story of Soulmates Stranded an Ocean Apart, by Kenneth P. Price, Ph.D.

The Man Across the River. The incredible story of one man's will to survive the Holocaust, by Zvi Wiesenfeld

If Anyone Calls, Tell Them I Died. A Memoir, by Emanuel (Manu) Rosen

The House on Thrömerstrasse. A Story of Rebirth and Renewal in the Wake of the Holocaust, by Ron Vincent

Dancing with my Father. His hidden past. Her quest for truth. How Nazi Vienna shaped a family's identity, by Jo Sorochinsky

The Story Keeper. Weaving the Threads of Time and Memory - A Memoir, by Fred Feldman

Krisia's Silence. The Girl who was not on Schindler's List, by Ronny Hein

Defying Death on the Danube. A Holocaust Survival Story, by Debbie J. Callahan with Henry Stern

A Doorway to Heroism. A decorated German-Jewish Soldier who became an American Hero, by Rabbi W. Jack Romberg

The Shoemaker's Son. The Life of a Holocaust Resister, by Laura Beth Bakst

The Redhead of Auschwitz. A True Story, by Nechama Birnbaum

Land of Many Bridges. My Father's Story, by Bela Ruth Samuel Tenenholtz

Creating Beauty from the Abyss. The Amazing Story of Sam Herciger, Auschwitz Survivor and Artist, by Lesley Ann Richardson

On Sunny Days We Sang. A Holocaust Story of Survival and Resilience, by Jeannette Grunhaus de Gelman

Painful Joy. A Holocaust Family Memoir, by Max J. Friedman

I Give You My Heart. A True Story of Courage and Survival, by Wendy Holden

In the Time of Madmen, by Mark A. Prelas

Monsters and Miracles. Horror, Heroes and the Holocaust, by Ira Wesley Kitmacher

Flower of Vlora. Growing up Jewish in Communist Albania, by Anna Kohen

Aftermath: Coming of Age on Three Continents. A Memoir, by Annette Libeskind Berkovits

Not a real Enemy. The True Story of a Hungarian Jewish Man's Fight for Freedom, by Robert Wolf

Zaidy's War. Four Armies, Three Continents, Two Brothers. One Man's Impossible Story of Endurance, by Martin Bodek

The Glassmaker's Son. Looking for the World my Father left behind in Nazi Germany, by Peter Kupfer

The Apprentice of Buchenwald. The True Story of the Teenage Boy Who Sabotaged Hitler's War Machine, by Oren Schneider

Good for a Single Journey, by Helen Joyce

Burying the Ghosts. She escaped Nazi Germany only to have her life torn apart by the woman she saved from the camps: her mother, by Sonia Case

American Wolf. From Nazi Refugee to American Spy. A True Story, by Audrey Birnbaum

Bipolar Refugee. A Saga of Survival and Resilience, by Peter Wiesner

Before the Beginning and After the End, by Hymie Anisman

Malka Owsiany recounts, by Mark Turkow (editor)

I Will Give Them an Everlasting Name. Jacksonville's Stories of the Holocaust, by Samuel P. Cox

The series **Jewish Children in the Holocaust** consists of the following autobiographies of Jewish children hidden during WWII in the Netherlands:

Searching for Home. The Impact of WWII on a Hidden Child, by Joseph Gosler

See You Tonight and Promise to be a Good Boy! War memories, by Salo Muller

Sounds from Silence. Reflections of a Child Holocaust Survivor, Psychiatrist and Teacher, by Robert Krell

Sabine's Odyssey. A Hidden Child and her Dutch Rescuers, by Agnes Schipper

The Journey of a Hidden Child, by Harry Pila and Robin Black

The series **New Jewish Fiction** consists of the following novels, written by Jewish authors. All novels are set in the time during or after the Holocaust.

The Corset Maker. A Novel, by Annette Libeskind Berkovits

Escaping the Whale. The Holocaust is over. But is it ever over for the next generation? by Ruth Rotkowitz

When the Music Stopped. Willy Rosen's Holocaust, by Casey Hayes

Hands of Gold. One Man's Quest to Find the Silver Lining in Misfortune, by Roni Robbins

The Girl Who Counted Numbers. A Novel, by Roslyn Bernstein

There was a garden in Nuremberg. A Novel, by Navina Michal Clemerson

The Butterfly and the Axe, by Omer Bartov

To Live Another Day. A Novel, Elizabeth Rosenberg

A Worthy Life. Based on a True Story, by Dahlia Moore

The series **Holocaust Heritage** consists of the following memoirs by 2G:

The Cello Still Sings. A Generational Story of the Holocaust and of the Transformative Power of Music, by Janet Horvath

The Fire and the Bonfire. A Journey into Memory, by Ardyn Halter

The Silk Factory: Finding Threads of My Family's True Holocaust Story, by Michael Hickins

Hidden in Plain Sight. A Journey into Memory and Place, by Julie Brill

Winter Light: The Memoir of a Child of Holocaust Survivors, by Grace Feuerverger

The series **Holocaust Books for Young Adults** consists of the following novels, based on true stories:

The Boy behind the Door. How Salomon Kool Escaped the Nazis. Inspired by a True Story, by David Tabatsky

Running for Shelter. A True Story, by Suzette Sheft

The Precious Few. An Inspirational Saga of Courage based on True Stories, by David Twain with Art Twain

The series **WWII Historical Fiction** consists of the following novels, some of which are based on true stories:

Mendelevski's Box. A Heartwarming and Heartbreaking Jewish Survivor's Story, by Roger Swindells

A Quiet Genocide. The Untold Holocaust of Disabled Children in WWII Germany, by Glenn Bryant

The Knife-Edge Path, by Patrick T. Leahy

Brave Face. The Inspiring WWII Memoir of a Dutch/German Child, by I. Caroline Crocker and Meta A. Evenbly

When We Had Wings. The Gripping Story of an Orphan in Janusz Korczak's Orphanage. A Historical Novel, by Tami Shem-Tov

Jacob's Courage. Romance and Survival amidst the Horrors of War, by Charles S. Weinblatt

Join the AP Review Team

Reviews are very important in a world dominated by the social media. Feedback for Holocaust books is more than just a customer review; it also shows the relevance and importance of such books in today's society.

Please go over to the AmsterdamPublishers.com website (top of page) if you want to join the *AP review team,* showing **at least one review on Amazon** for one of our books. You will get updates about new releases and will get the chance to read and review.

www.ingramcontent.com/pod-product-compliance
Lightning Source LLC
LaVergne TN
LVHW041708070526
838199LV00045B/1252